This Far By Faith:

My Journey Through Life Guided By My Faith

Trudy N. Stiff

This Far By Faith
© 2021 by Trudy N. Stiff

All rights reserved. No portion of this publication may be reproduced, stored in a retrieval system, or transmitted in any form or by any means-electronic, mechanical, photocopying, recording, scanning, or other-except for brief quotations in critical reviews or articles, without the prior written permission of the publisher.

Published in Hampton, VA, by Fruition Publishing Concierge Services. Fruition Publishing Concierge Services is a division of Alesha Brown, LLC.

Fruition Publishing Concierge Services can bring authors to your live event. For more information or to book an event, visit Fruition Publishing Concierge Services at

www.FruitionPublishing.com

ISBN: 978-1-954486-33-1 Paperback

ISBN: 978-1-954486-34-8 eBook

Library of Congress Control Number: 2021918112

Unless otherwise noted, all scriptures are from The Holy Bible, King James Version. (2004). Dallas, TX: Brown Books Publishing.

Trudy N. Stiff is the epitome of ***I don't look like what I've been through***. This Far By Faith takes you on a personal and transparent journey of how she overcame many life obstacles simply by faith. She takes you through the highs and lows of childhood, family ties, love, life, death, and so much more.

This book helps you not only show empathy for others but also provides a benchmark for your own faith walk. The inserted scriptures serve as a resource so that you can have a starting point if you are faced with similar situations.

The confidence in which this book is written creates a self-assurance that you can truly trust God and continue to walk through life by faith. I am encouraged and inspired by her words and perseverance. This book is a refreshing reminder to strengthen your relationship with God and connect to His word.

Kathy Taylor
Author|Speaker|Coach
Kathy Taylor Consulting, LLC

As if propelled on invisible wings, readers will effortlessly glide over page by page of This Far By Faith. Not only is this a story of pain and loss through the years that would break even the strongest person, but it is also a testament of one woman's strong faith in God's abiding love.

A truly delightful book, **This Far By Faith** will stay with you long after you turn the very last page.

Carol Gee, M.A.

Author of the "girlfriend books" The Venus Chronicles, Random Notes, etc.

This was truly a pleasure for me to read and evoked feelings of warmth from inspiration and reminders of parts of my family history. So often, we pass by landmarks, well-known streets, and historical areas but are completely oblivious of the rich history contained therein. Mrs. Stiff's depiction of her upbringing and wisdom shared from her parents and family reminded me of some of my family's history and words of wisdom.

In these times, we all need inspiration, and Mrs. Stiff is the epitome of that and then some. We hear and know about how our faith can carry us through, but when you hear all her challenges and adversities, you will wonder how one person can manage to have the grace, positivity, and strength that she does. There are some heart-stopping, painful moments, but your soul will be on fire through every twist and turn.

My heart is thrilled that Mrs. Stiff took the time to record the awe that is her life and God's hands and blessings that have been over her life and still is. I hope this book will be used as a conversation piece within families to discuss their history, obstacles, and timeless and invaluable wisdom.

Alesha Brown, The Joy Guru
CEO, Fruition Publishing Concierge Services
Publisher|Speaker|Award-Winning Entrepreneur

Dedication

This book is dedicated first and foremost to my Lord and Savior, Jesus Christ, who is the head of my life and the reason for my existence.

I also dedicate this book to my parents, Deacon Milton and Deaconess Minnie Nelson. They were my first role models of a Godly husband and father and a Godly wife and mother. They began teaching me about faith and God during my formative years. Because of their example and teaching, I have grown into the woman of God that I am today. For that, I am so grateful!

Table Of Contents

Walking by faith with my Daddy 5

Walking by faith with Mama 17

Finding love and marriage by faith 27

Walking by faith while becoming parents 49

Walking by faith through a "new normal" 71

Walking by faith during the onset of illnesses 79

Walking by faith through the fires 101

Walking by faith through a second chance at love 115

About the Author 137

Prologue

My life up until now has become my past. However, as a new chapter begins, let us see what God has in store for me next. Whatever it may be, I will walk through it by faith. I made it this far by trusting in God's word, leaning on Him, trusting Him who is infallible. Thank you, Lord!

Background

I was born into a Christian family. My great-grandfather was a minister, my Daddy was a deacon in the church, and my Mama was a deaconess. As a child, I went to Sunday school, then morning service, followed by BTU (Baptist Training Union) for the church's children. We learned about the bible through social interactions such as playing games, group discussions, watching movies, and other similar activities. These activities made it fun as we learned about God's word and how to develop our faith. After leaving there, we went straight into Sunday night worship service.

I was baptized at the age of five alongside my sister, who was six years old. I was a member of the junior choir as well as the junior ushers. As I got older, I was a member of the youth choir, the senior choir, and the joint choir. I was also a member of a service organization called the Perry Madison League. We were the food preparers and Hospitality Committee for the church.

I was also a Sunday school teacher for several years and the pianist for Sunday school. I was also a Vacation Bible School teacher and usually worked with the toddler class. As you can see, I was well-grounded in the church.

My faith grew stronger as I got older and encountered this thing that we call LIFE! Hence, the title of this book: THIS FAR BY FAITH.

FAITH

My life is all
God's plan
He has it in the palm of
His hand

Whatever situations
May arise
He is always
By my side

My faith looks up
To thee
Oh lamb of
Calvary

Your promises
Are true
I put my faith and trust
In you

You've been there
From the beginning
With you
There is no ending

I owe my life
To you
You are first in all
That I do

My faith will never
Waver
Because you are my
Lord and Savior.

Trudy Nelson Stiff

Walking by faith with my Daddy

My Daddy, Deacon Milton Stanley Nelson Sr., was a proud but humble man. He only had a seventh-grade education, leaving school at a young age to help out with the family. However, he prided himself on learning things on his own. As the years passed, Daddy became a businessman.

Becoming the founder and proud owner of Nelson's Barber Shop in the Titustown area of Norfolk, Virginia, this business existed for about 43 years. Daddy prided himself in having a wholesome, family-friendly business. He demanded that women who brought their young children in for haircuts be respected. No inappropriate language, conversations or actions, were tolerated in or around his business.

Daddy had a sign up in his barbershop that said: "Be Nice or Be Gone." He was fully committed to that rule. If you didn't abide by the rules or act appropriately, then you were asked to leave. This did not present a problem because Daddy was very well respected, and his business and reputation had made a name for itself.

Daddy wore a shirt and tie to the barbershop every day. He put his barber smock over it, but he believed strongly in being neat and looking professional.

Daddy was also a very active member of our church, the First Baptist Church of Logan Park. Selected to be a deacon there, he took this role very seriously.   1 Timothy 3: 8-10, KJV says:

> "Likewise, must the deacons be grave, not double tongued, not given to much wine, not greedy of filthy lucre;
>
> Holding the mystery of the faith in a pure conscience. And let these also first be proved; then let them use the office of a deacon, being found blameless."

Daddy really loved God, and he taught us to love God also. He taught his four daughters to be respectable young ladies. One of his favorite phrases was "be a lady."

Daddy also used to mentor some of the boys in the neighborhood. He would often talk to them about how to be young gentlemen and to have respect for themselves. From time to time, he hired a few of them to help around the barbershop with sweeping up, taking out the trash, etc. This gave them a little money in their pockets and helped them to feel good about themselves.

My Daddy was also very protective of us and had strict rules about where we could and could not go. At the time, I felt that he was too strict because some of the other kids could go places that we were not allowed.

Now that we are grown and have children of our own, we often talk about how we appreciate the way we were raised. As a matter of fact, we have tried to emulate what we were taught. Ephesians 6:4 says:

> "And, ye fathers, provoke not your children to wrath: but bring them up in the nurture and admonition of the Lord."

My sister that is next to me in age, and I often chuckle when we see some of the guys from our childhood. They say to us, "We didn't dare try to talk to or date you Nelson girls because your Daddy didn't play!"

If there was such a thing as a "perfect" model of a Godly husband and father, my Daddy was it. He was a quiet and mild-mannered man. I don't ever recall hearing him raise his voice in an argumentative or angry way, but he had a way of talking to you (almost preaching) that if you had done something wrong, made you feel so bad that you would rather he had spanked you.

I never received a spanking from my Daddy. I was an obedient child and did not want to disappoint him. When any of us did something wrong, we could see the disappointment on his face. Ephesians 6:1 says:

"Children obey your parents in the Lord, for this is right."

Daddy wanted the best for his children. There were eight of us: four boys and four girls. My sister that's one year older than I am, and I came along late in life for my parents. When we came along, the youngest child at that time was 14 years old.

Because he was not able to get a formal education, Daddy really believed in one. He wanted us to be educated and as well-rounded and prepared for life as possible. Growing up, we were Girl Scouts, and we participated in church youth organizations, including the choir and the usher board. We also participated in Christmas and Easter plays and any other special program that came up.

We were in the Girl Scouts for several years. I belonged to a bowling team, the SCA (student council association), and a social/service club called the Keyetts. During my senior year in high school, I was voted into the Hall of Fame as the "friendliest."

Daddy was very proud because he always taught us to be kind to everyone. He also taught us that we were not better than anyone, but we were just as good as the next person.

Daddy encouraged us to take piano and organ lessons, which we did for several years. We had an organ in the living room of our home and a piano in the dining room. My sister was the substitute organist at church once in a while, and I played for the Sunday school as an adult. Proverbs 22:6 says:

"Train up a child in the way he should go, and when he is old he will not depart from it."

We took piano lessons from a lady in the neighborhood, and every year we participated in a recital. We played separate songs, but it was a tradition that my sister and I always played a duet at the recital. Mama and Daddy were so proud; you could see it on their faces.

I appreciate Daddy's sacrifices because I know that it was not easy giving us the extra things that he did. I can truly say growing up as a child, I didn't feel we were deprived of anything.

Daddy only wanted the best for us. Even as a young child, I remember going to one of the better shoe stores because he always said it was very important to have good, sturdy shoes for your feet.

Daddy was a very generous and giving man. I can remember occasions when we were going places in the car with him, and he would see someone less fortunate and stop the car to see what he could do to help.

He always kept a spare pair of shoes in the car's trunk because he would wear one pair to work and then change into a more comfortable pair later when he would have to do a lot of standing.

I will never forget when we were driving down the street, and there was a person who was probably homeless (you could tell that he was down-on-his-luck, as he had shoes on his feet that had visible holes in them). Daddy went around the corner and parked the car. He then went into the trunk and got the pair of shoes he always kept there and gave them to the man. That is the kind of person he was. Matthew 25:36 says:

> "Naked, and ye clothed me: I was sick, and ye visited me: I was in prison, and ye came unto me."

Verse 40 says:

> "And the King shall answer and say unto them, Verily I say unto you, in as much as ye have done it unto one of the least of these my brethren, ye have done it unto me."

One of the many jobs that Daddy performed as a church deacon was to fix the announcement board on the outside of the church. He used to take my sister and me with him sometimes, so we could pick out the letters to the words and hand them to him.

This was his way of testing our spelling skills. I smile when I think of this because Daddy used everything as an opportunity to teach us something. He would also ask us questions that would require us to think.

If we were riding down the street, he would say, "Okay, read that sign to me." Or he would quiz us on certain things such as multiplication or division, etc. He just wanted us to be sharp and quick thinking. Talking to my Daddy, you would never have known that he hadn't gone any farther than he went in school.

For example, he kept up on current events. He was always reading and loved to watch documentaries on TV. With the help of the Lord and with God's favor, he truly became an educated man.

He was also very interested in politics and was nominated and elected as one of the Norfolk Virginia Citizen's Advisory Committee members. He really took pride in that position and worked very hard to better our city and communities. We were so proud of him.

Daddy worked hard all of his life, and as the last two of us girls got older and near college-age, he took on an additional job. He got a job at night working at the grain elevator near the Norfolk Naval Base.

That's where the trains came in loaded with cargo that had to be unloaded and stored. I didn't know at that time that one of the reasons he took that job was to buy both my sister and me a car. My sister would be leaving for college in a year, and I would be leaving the following year.

The cars Daddy bought us weren't brand new, but as he said, "they were nice, sturdy cars that were safe." I was so happy to be getting a car that I didn't care what it looked like.

Both of our cars were nice-looking, used cars, and he prided himself in making sure to have them checked out so that his girls would not be out with the car breaking down on us.

Time went on, and we both went away to two different schools. My sister went to Hampton Institute (now known as Hampton

University), and a year later, I went to Virginia State College (now known as Virginia State University).

If you can't tell yet, yes, I was a Daddy's girl. That is why it hurt me so much when we started seeing signs of deterioration in him. By that time, my older brothers and sisters were all grown up and married, and some were living away. The last two of us girls were also married by then. All four of us girls and one of our brothers were living in Norfolk.

Mama had started to notice that Daddy was becoming a bit forgetful. He had stopped working his second job some years back, however, he was still working at the barbershop.

My brother, who lived in Norfolk, had left the Merchant Seaman's and worked at the barbershop with him. There were also two other barbers working there with him that had been there for years. We felt pretty comfortable knowing that my brother was working alongside him and could keep an eye on him.

As time passed, Daddy's condition worsened. He was beginning to show some signs that concerned us, so we took him to the doctor. After a series of tests, we were told that he was showing the early signs of dementia.

The plan at that time was to continue to allow him to work, drive, and be as independent as possible since my brother was there to keep an eye on him. This continued for a couple of years until Daddy got to the point that he started doing things such as leaving the house when Mama was asleep in the middle of the night. On several occasions, Mama called us and told us that he had left the house and she didn't know where he was.

Mama didn't drive, and she didn't need to be out looking for him anyway, so my husband and I would go out looking for him. Or my sister and her husband or my brother would. Sometimes, we all went out at the same time, each selecting a different area to drive around and look for him. We would always manage to find him, by the grace of God, and he was always okay. Thank you, Lord!

One night, I remember distinctly at 3 a.m., when my husband and I found him parked on the side of the road with the car windows rolled up, the doors locked, and sound asleep. We had to knock on the window to wake him up. He had no idea where he was and did not remember leaving the house. Psalms 46:1 says:

> "God is our refuge and strength, a very present help in trouble."

There were a couple of more incidences of this happening, so we had a family meeting and determined that Daddy needed to stop driving and working. We knew that this would be difficult for him, but it had become a safety issue. We had a meeting with Daddy and discussed our concerns with him.

God is good because he accepted it much better than we thought he would. We assured him that one of us would be available to take him wherever he needed to go.

He wanted my husband to have his car, although my husband had his own truck. We made sure that we drove his car whenever we took Daddy somewhere because it made him feel good to see that his car was still running and being taken care of. Daddy had always taken pride in keeping his car neat and clean and in good running condition.

About a year or so later, Daddy's thought processes seemed to decline a little bit more, and the doctor said that he was in early-onset Alzheimer's. Mama, at the time, was having some health issues of her own, and my sisters, brother, and I were all still working full-time. A couple of us even had small children.

What we decided to do was take turns spending the night with our parents. That way, we could keep an eye on Daddy so that he would not leave the house and go walking somewhere by himself at night.

We did this for a while, and then Mama ended up in the hospital with some serious health issues. When it was almost time for her to be discharged, the doctor told her that she needed to make some decisions about Daddy because she was no longer physically able to care for him at home.

Reluctantly, we had another family meeting. It broke all our hearts, but we decided that we needed to look into putting Daddy into a nursing facility. He was now at the point of needing 24-hour supervision. The thought of our Daddy, who had always been so independent and thrived on helping and doing for others was now becoming dependent on someone else, was heartbreaking.

One of the things that Daddy used to do on Wednesdays when the barbershop was closed was going to the homes of the sick and shut-in of the church and our community and cut their hair. That was one of the hardest things for him to accept when he could no longer drive. We certainly did not want him to feel useless by having to move into a facility. We knew, however, that we had to do what was best for his safety.

We were blessed to find a newly built nursing facility right there in Norfolk that had just begun to take in residents. Daddy was one of the first occupants to move into the brand, new facility. Other than arthritis, Daddy had no other physical ailments, so he was truly blessed. It was only his mind that was not functioning so well.

Those who lived in Norfolk and the Virginia Beach area were regularly there to ensure that he was well cared for. We'd heard many different stories about how nursing facilities could be, and we were not going to accept anything but the best for our Daddy. After all, he had always provided the best for us.

We would also go and get Daddy for holidays, sometimes on the weekends or his birthday, and take him out to eat or to one of our homes. We could see a gradual decline over the years, but God allowed him eight years of living in that facility and being able to enjoy his family before he passed away.

Daddy passed away on August 27, 1997, which was also my sister's birthday. He was 80 years old. Micah 6:8 says:

> "He hath shewed thee, O man, what is good; and what doth the LORD requires of thee, but to do justly, and to love mercy, and to walk humbly with thy God."

Thank you, Lord, for a God-fearing Daddy. I love and miss you!

Walking by faith with Mama

Although my Mama was short in stature, she was a strong and determined woman of God who refused to let life get her down. Mama's mother passed away when she was 12 years old. At the time, she was the oldest sibling, the only girl, and had three younger brothers.

My Granddaddy worked at the shipyard, so Mama was responsible for getting herself and the boys off to school daily. When she returned home from school, she would make sure that everyone got their homework done, that dinner was prepared, and the house was taken care of.

Mama never spoke negatively about this time in her life, although I'm sure it was difficult for her. After all, she was still a child herself, having to help raise her brothers, which couldn't have been easy. She always told us that Granddaddy provided well for them, so she did not mind helping at home.

My Granddaddy was also a strong man of God, as his father had been a preacher. That is where my Mama got her religious roots. They were instilled in her, and she, in turn, instilled them in us.

They were required to attend church on Sundays and were taught to remember the Sabbath day and keep it holy. Exodus 34:21 says:

> "Six days thou shalt work, but on the seventh day thou shalt rest: in earning time and in harvest time thou shalt rest."

Sundays were for worship, honoring God, as well as a time to be with family. There was no doing laundry, housework, or anything other than cooking on Sunday if the meal had not been completely prepared on Saturday.

The boys were typical boys. They used to play roughhouse and wrestle, but they were very respectful of their sister. When asked to do something by Mama, they usually did as she said. Granddaddy was a strict disciplinarian and also expected them to do as they were told.

The situation was not an easy one but seemed to work well for their family during that time. Mama always told us that things don't always go smoothly in life, yet you must do the best that you can with the circumstances that God gives you. She always said that "If God brings you to it, then He will bring you through it. Just keep your faith and trust in Him."

As time passed, they grew older, and the boys went on to different careers, got married, and had families. Mama met a man, fell in love, and got married. She had two sons from that union that only lasted a few years until they divorced. After that, Mama worked in a school cafeteria and continued raising her two boys.

Eventually, she met a handsome young man who was a widower with four small children. He had two boys and two little girls. This man became my Daddy because he and Mama fell in love, married, and merged their two families. Between the two of them, they had six children: four boys and two girls.

Daddy moved his new family to the Titustown area of Norfolk. Leaning on his faith and trust in God, he opened up his barbershop. The business did well and the family blended well. Mama was a happy wife and mother to all six of the children. Jeremiah 29:11: says:

> "For I know the thoughts that I think toward you, saith the LORD, thoughts of peace, and not of evil, to give you an expected end."

When the youngest of the six turned 14 years old, Mama found out she was expecting another little bundle of joy. This would be my sister. When my sister was four months old, Mama found out that she was expecting another bundle of joy! Guess who? That's right, me! I was now the baby, and the family had grown to a total of eight children: four boys and four girls. Psalms 127:3 says:

> "Lo, children are a heritage of the LORD: and the fruit of the womb is his reward."

By the time we came along, all of my brothers and my oldest sister were out of the house. Two brothers went to the military, one to the Navy and one to the Air Force. Another brother became a Merchant Seaman, and the fourth brother went away to college and eventually became a New York City firefighter. My oldest sister got married and got a job at the Norfolk Naval Base, where she worked until she retired.

So out of the six older sisters and brothers, the youngest of them was still at home. Our older sister obtained a job at one of the local hospitals and worked there for 42 years until she retired.

She often tells a story of how we were like her babies, and she helped take care of us and changed our diapers, combed our hair, gave us our bottles, and played with us. She said she enjoyed helping to take care of us. She enjoyed spoiling us and, sometimes, reminded us to this day that she is still the big sister, lol!

In the meantime, Granddaddy had met a nice lady and married her. She was the only Grandma that I have ever known. They had two daughters of their own. For the first time in her life, my Mom had sisters. She loved her younger sisters, and they loved her. We got to know our new Grandmother and Aunties very well and went to visit them often. We all grew to be very close.

Every Easter, we looked forward to going to Grandma's house because she would always get my sister and me a big chocolate Easter egg made with our names on them. My sister always wanted coconut, and I liked the fruit and nut. This was an Easter tradition for us, but we liked going to Grandma's and Granddaddy's house any time just to visit. It did not have to be a special occasion.

It felt good to have a Grandmother because both Mama and Daddy's mothers were deceased. After a few years, Granddaddy got sick and eventually passed away. It was a sad time for us all. However, God is true to His word, and he saw Mama through the death of her father as well as Grandma through the death of her husband.

God is faithful. John 14:1 says:

> "Let not your heart be troubled: ye believe in God, believe also in me."

John 14:18 says:

> "I will not leave you comfortless: I will come to you."

As time passed, both of my Aunties got married and began having families of their own. Sometimes we would go on family outings to the park. Grandma, my Aunts, and their families would also go. My Grandma loved Kentucky Fried Chicken, so my Mama would always make sure we had some for her. And you best believe that Grandma would specify that she wanted extra crispy!

After several years, Grandma passed away. By that time, we were all married with our own families. Mama's health also began to fail. She was living alone at that time because we had to put Daddy in a nursing facility due to his Alzheimer's progressing, and she could no longer care for him.

Mama had high blood pressure, diabetes, heart issues, and eventually developed end-stage renal disease and started dialysis. We were all concerned about her living by herself.

My husband lovingly called her Mother Nelson. One day, after work, we were sitting down eating dinner, and my husband said to me, "I think we should bring Mother Nelson here to live with us." This brought tears to my eyes. However, I really wasn't surprised because that was the kind of man that my husband was.

My husband was loving, kind, and giving. He always showed love towards my Mother, and she loved him dearly. Theirs was never one of the horrific mother-in-law scenarios that you often hear.

We talked about it, and I told him that I would not want him to feel uncomfortable in his own home or that he had to be a caregiver. He told me that neither of those things would be a problem because he remembered how I helped his mother when she got ill. I thank God for sending me that man. I did not choose him; God chose him for me.

How blessed I was that my husband had such love for me and such concern for my Mother that he would suggest that and not feel that he was sacrificing anything. Thank you, Lord, for the man you chose for me! 2 Corinthians 6:14 says:

> "Be not unequally yoked together with unbelievers for what fellowship hath righteousness with unrighteousness? And what communion hath light with darkness?"

After talking and praying about it, we began planning our schedules to get my mother to and from her dialysis treatments once she began living with us. The next day, we talked to Mama about it. She was overjoyed and readily accepted. Personally, I think she had been a little apprehensive about living on her own with her health declining, so the suggestion was a great comfort to her.

We moved Mama in with us, and things progressed well. My siblings came by to visit and help in any way that they could. Herbert (my husband) and I worked out a schedule between the two of us to transport her to and from her dialysis treatments because we definitely did not want her on the bus. Exodus 20:12 says:

> "Honour thy father and thy mother: that thy days may be long upon the land which the LORD thy God giveth thee."

Things went smoothly for several months. Then, on March 15, 1995, Herbert and I went into the bedroom to change our clothes after picking up Mama from dialysis. Herbert told Mama to sit down at the dining room table because he had started preparing dinner before we left to pick her up. In the meantime, Herbert got a phone call from his sister and was on the phone talking to her while he was in the kitchen.

When I came out of the bedroom, I noticed that Mama was sitting in the chair at the head of the table with her head slumped over backward. Her eyes were closed, and her mouth was open. I said, "Mama, Mama." She did not respond, so I shook her. Still no response. Having been trained in CPR for my job, I put my ear and cheek to her mouth to see if I could hear and feel any breathing, but I couldn't.

I then pulled her out of the chair and laid her on the floor, yelling for Herbert to get off the phone with his sister and call 911. I began to perform CPR. I continued breaths and compressions until the paramedics got there. It did not take them long to get there, thank God. They took over for me as Herbert tried to comfort me.

I just kept saying, "No Lord, not my Mama, not my Mama, Lord." My Mama was my best friend. I could talk to her about anything. She was my "ride or die" buddy.

The paramedics put her on a stretcher and took her out of the house while still working on her. They told us what hospital they were going to, and Herbert and I called my siblings and told them what happened as we made our way over to the hospital.

Before we arrived, I knew that God had called her home. A calmness came over me, and I heard God whisper in my ear, "She is with me now. She has come home."

When we arrived at the ER, my sisters, brother-in-law, and brother arrived soon afterward. The nurses ushered us into a private room, they told us that the doctor would be with us shortly. We all knew what that meant.

We were incredibly sad and emotional when the doctor came in and told us that they had done all that they could but were unable to save her. 2 Corinthians 5:8 says:

> "We are confident, I say, and willing rather to be absent from the body, and to be present with the Lord."

We were all quite saddened by the passing of our Mama, but we knew that she was in a better place. She would not have to endure any more pain or suffering, and, for that, we were grateful. She had prepared us for this day, always saying to us that "no one lives forever" and "what you need to be sure of is when your time comes, will you make it through the Pearly Gates?"

Mama had a beautiful homegoing service. We all wore white dresses in honor of her because she had always said she did not want a lot of black, dark, and mournful colors when she left this earth. After Mama's death, I also started a tradition of buying pretty lace handkerchiefs for all of us daughters and daughter-in-laws to have at the funeral. Mama always kept beautiful lace handkerchiefs that she would carry to church with her on Sundays. We kept this tradition when my Daddy passed, as well as when my older sister passed.

Our family has always been close-knit, interwoven, and intertwined by the love of our Mama and Daddy. They both taught us what was right, and we received it and continue to live it to this day. Ephesians 6:1 says:

"Children obey your parents in the Lord for this is right."

It was truly faith in God and knowing that He keeps His word that got me through the death of my Mama.

The words from the Virtuous Woman scripture in Proverbs 31 spoke of my Mama. Verses 27-31 say:

"She looketh well to the ways of her household, and eateth not the bread of idleness. Her children arise up, and call her blessed; her husband also, and he praiseth her. Many daughters have done virtuously, but thou excellest them all. Favor is deceitful, and beauty is vain: but a woman that feareth the LORD, she shall be praised. Give her of the fruit of her hands; and let her own works praise her in the gates."

I love and miss you, Mama! I describe my Mother (Mama) in the following way:

M	Magnificent Creation of God
O	Overflowing with Love
T	The epitome of the Virtuous Woman
H	Heaven's Sweetest Angel
E	Earth's Greatest Asset
R	Reserved in My Heart Forever

Finding love and marriage by faith

Herbert Eugene Stiff was a kind, pleasant, and jovial man. He was large in stature, about 6 feet 2 inches tall, and about 275 lbs. His personality was just as large as his stature. He was a man who had never met a stranger. Little did I know when we first met that it was in God's plan that he and I would eventually become united in holy matrimony.

Herbert served in the US Army and did a tour of duty during the Vietnam War. He intended to make a career of the military, but once he found out he would be required to do another tour of active duty in Vietnam, he decided against it.

During the war, he flew what they called Medivac (he was in the helicopters that went into the jungles to pick up the wounded soldiers). He said that God allowed him to serve and make it out uninjured and alive the first time, so he was not willing to risk it again.

I remember him telling me that he did not drink coffee because he had a cup of hot coffee in his hands the first time his camp was attacked. He said that his heart was racing, and he was petrified. The coffee spilled all over him as he jumped up to take cover, and, after that, he could no longer drink coffee. I'm sure it reminded him of that first traumatic experience in Vietnam that he did not want to relive.

At the end of his Tour of Duty, Herbert was honorably discharged and returned home. Psalm 91:11 says:

> "For he shall give his angels charge over thee, to keep thee in all thy ways."

That is exactly what he did for Herbert. He dispatched His angels to watch over him continuously during his Tour of Duty. Thank you, Lord! Your promises are true.

When Herbert returned home, he went into the bricklaying trade. He loved working outdoors, and he loved building, creating things, and working with his hands. He went into an apprenticeship and learned the trade from a family friend who was also one of his church members. During that time, they constructed many commercial buildings, homes, and many of the 7-Eleven stores. Herbert thoroughly enjoyed his job and his co-workers, some with whom he became close friends.

Herbert was an extremely hard worker, so during the off-season for construction work or when the weather was too cold, he would get fill-in jobs. After all, 2 Thessalonians 3:10 says:

"For even when we were with you, this we commanded you, that if any would not work, neither should he eat."

Well, Herbert loved to eat, so he definitely did not mind working. He also turned out to be a good cook.

When Herbert entered my life, I had left college and was working at Southeastern Virginia Training Center. While I had majored in special education, my desire wasn't to teach in a classroom. My concern was for the developmentally disabled who lived in institutions and did not get the opportunity to live at home with their parents and loved ones. That desire grew in me during my schooling and visiting state institutions like Eastern State Hospital and Central State Hospital.

I found my place at Southeastern Virginia Training Center located in Chesapeake, Virginia. It was a residential facility for the developmentally disabled. It was a perfect fit for me because it was a home-like setting for the residents. They lived on a campus designed with individual houses that were called cottages.

Each cottage housed eight to ten residents, with one to two people sharing a bedroom decorated with nice curtains, comforters, and other items, to make their environment home-like.

Each cottage also had a living room, a fully equipped kitchen, three bathrooms, residential space for a staff member, a storage area, and an office area. One residential unit was twice the size of the other cottages, so everything there was doubled.

There was also an administration building, a gymnasium, and a cafeteria on the campus. At that time, Herbert had also taken a job there, working in the cafeteria and delivering meals to the different cottages and housing units. He would bring prepared meals from the cafeteria three times a day.

Minding my own business, working with the other staff and residents, I noticed that another man had come in with a co-worker I was familiar with. This man was new.

I heard the new man say to his coworker, "Doesn't she have a beautiful smile?" I began to notice that he said it every time he came in and sometimes would add, "And she's always smiling." The first few times, I didn't pay him much attention. I heard what he said but continued doing what I was doing.

I really didn't think anything of it. But then he made it his business to say this three times a day, or each time he would enter the cottage. Finally, I asked, "Are you talking about me?" And he said," Yes, didn't you know?" I said, "No, I didn't until I noticed you were looking directly at me when you said it this last time."

Well, I guess that opened the door for him because after that, every time he came into the cottage, he would find something to say to me specifically. Eventually, he asked me for my phone number. I was not one to give out my information readily, so I asked him, "Why don't you give me your phone number, and I will think about it. And maybe then I will give you a call, and we can talk."

He readily gave me his number, and I kept it for about a week or two. We, however, continued to talk whenever he would come into the cottage.

One Friday, I decided to call him. We talked briefly because I had questions that I needed answers to, such as, Are you married? Have you ever been married? Do you have children? And do you have a current lady?

He answered those questions satisfactorily, so I gave him my phone number and told him to call me sometime. I forgot to mention that I had no idea what his name was when he came into the cottage those first few times. When I asked him if he was talking to me, I finally asked, "What is your name? You're new here because I've only seen you coming around recently." That is when I learned that his name was Herbert Stiff.

Herbert called me the very next day and asked me out to dinner. I agreed to go to dinner with him, and we went out and sat and talked for hours. We talked about our backgrounds and our lives up until that point.

We talked about our parents, our Christian beliefs, and many other things. We discovered that we had a lot of things in common, particularly our belief in God. I let him know that was especially important to me in a relationship with any man. The one difference in our religious backgrounds was that he was brought up in the Episcopal Church but was an active member of the AME (African Methodist Episcopal) Church.

I was brought up Baptist and was still a practicing Baptist. This wasn't really a problem because we both believed in God and the teachings of the Bible. We both also believed that God must be the head of the household.

Going to church was a must for me, and being an active participant in the church was also a must. Having children and raising them in the church was extremely important. He was an "old school" type of man and possessed many of my values. He believed in opening doors, pulling out chairs for ladies, and removing his hat when in a building and those types of things. These were the types of things that Daddy taught me a long time ago that a real man who was a gentleman should do. Therefore, these were things that I expected.

We dated for a while and, during that time, I got to meet his family. He and his mother were very close, and he was very close to his siblings. He had an older brother who was married and a sister. He was the baby of the family.

I also introduced him to my family during this time. Mama and Daddy met him first. They seemed to take to his warm and engaging personality readily. When I asked their opinion of him, they told me that he was respectful, God-fearing, and seemed to have been raised well. Eventually, he met my siblings, and they liked him right away. Herbert was the type of man that met no strangers and made you feel comfortable the moment that you met him.

He was also very comical and loved to joke. We continued dating and sometimes would double date with my sister, a year older than me, and her boyfriend. In the meantime, I had been praying and asking God what He was trying to show me. Was he doing something new and different in my life with this person? After all, Matthew 7:7 says:

> "Ask, and it shall be given you; seek, and ye shall find; knock, and it shall be opened unto you."

Our relationship became serious after dating for about a year. His family had a tradition of going to church with his brother's family every Christmas Eve. Following the church service, they would all go back to the brother's house, and everyone got to open one gift. Herbert invited me to go with him in December of 1981.

When we got to the house, everyone took a turn opening a gift. It was a very festive time, and I was enjoying all of the excitement. I was not expecting to be included in the gift exchange because this was their tradition. After everyone had opened a gift, Herbert said, "There is one more gift to be opened."

He came over to me, pulled a little black velvet box out of his pocket, and handed it to me. As I opened the box, my eyes got big as golf balls to discover a beautiful diamond engagement ring. He asked me would I marry him and become part of his family and their Christmas tradition.

I was so happy, and of course, I said yes! Everyone was extremely excited and happy for us. His family had already made me feel as if I were a part of the family anyway, so this made it just perfect.

During our courtship, I prayed to God and asked him to show me if this was the person He had for me. Herbert was ten years older than me, but he treated me so well. In the previous chapter about my Daddy, you may remember that he taught his girls how a man should treat them.

Well, I must say Herbert fit the description. He believed in being a protector, a provider, and just making his lady happy. He was also active in his church. He was an usher and was in both the male and senior choir. All these things were important to me, and God had provided the man that I needed. 1 Corinthians 7:2 says:

> "Nevertheless, to avoid fornication, let every man have his own wife, and let every woman have her own husband."

Herbert and I set a wedding date and went about planning. We didn't have long because we became engaged in December and set the wedding for July. We were both anxious to start our life together as husband and wife. We enjoyed being around each other and were anxious to make it permanent.

My Mama used to say, "When you get to the point that you don't want him to leave and go home, then it's time to go on and marry him."

Herbert and I were married on July 3rd, 1982, at my church, First Baptist Church of Logan Park. Proverbs 18:22 says:

"Whoso findeth a wife findeth a good thing, and obtaineth favour of the LORD."

It was a bright and sunny day. It was also quite hot outside, however, that didn't bother me a bit. I was both excited and nervous. The thought of walking down the aisle in front of all of those people was a bit unnerving.

However, it was a beautiful wedding. My colors were rainbow. I chose those colors because I like bright colors and, after all, it was a summer wedding. My choice of rainbow colors was a bit untraditional because my favorite color was red, and I wanted my sister, who was my maid of honor, to wear red. I consulted my wedding director and asked her would it be appropriate to include red in my rainbow. She told me that it was my wedding and that I could have whatever colors I wanted.

My rainbow consisted of red, yellow, light blue, pink, light green, lavender, and orange. The girls looked so pretty lined up at the altar. I had seven attendants; five were friends from college. My sister was the maid of honor, and my niece was a junior bridesmaid.

Herbert had seven groomsmen, two of them friends of mine from college. The others were his friends, and his brother was his best man. Each groomsman wore off-white tuxedos with a carnation in the lapel to color coordinate with the bridesmaid's dress that he was escorting.

Herbert wore an off-white tuxedo with tails. He looked so handsome standing with the Pastor and his groomsmen as my Daddy walked me down the aisle.

The church was filled to capacity! I had sent out over two hundred invitations trying not to exclude anyone. A reception followed in the church annex. I was especially happy because some of our co-workers attended and were able to bring some of the residents that we cared for. It was important to me that they could share on this joyful occasion.

Herbert and I enjoyed a wonderful marriage. People often find it hard to believe when I tell them that we did not argue. Of course, we did not agree on everything, but we talked things out and compromised on issues.

Neither Herbert nor I were argumentative people. We both had peaceful spirits. I do not ever remember him raising his voice to me, nor I to him. That's just the way that we were. Those that know me know that I am non-confrontational and non-argumentative.

Eventually, I decided to join Herbert's church. He and I had been alternating attending each other's church together. We talked about needing to decide which church would become the church that we attended regularly.

He was more than willing to leave his church and come to mine, but I told him that I would give membership at his church a try. My reason for that was he was a man who was working diligently in several capacities at his church, and I did not want to mess with that. Often, it is hard even to get a man to go to church, not to mention being as actively involved as he was. Also, I had been away at college for four years, so I had only recently returned to my church as an active member. Joshua 24:15 says:

> "And if it seem evil unto you to serve the Lord, choose you this day whom ye will serve; whether the gods which your fathers served that were on the other side of the flood, or the gods of the Amorites, in whose land ye dwell; but as for me and my house, we will serve the Lord."

Our life progressed very well. Herbert had returned to bricklaying, and I was still at my job. By then, praise God, I had been promoted as a shift supervisor. After working in that capacity for about a year, an opening became available for a building supervisor. I applied for the position, interviewed, and was chosen. To God be the glory!

After about five years of marriage, we had not yet conceived a child. However, there were two opportunities that we had to adopt children. We accepted both and adopted one son in 1987 and another in 1995.

When our first son, Desmond, was about three years old, I got a bit homesick for my Baptist roots. I wanted him to experience some of the things that we did with our youth in the church. He had been experiencing the AME side, so now I wanted to show him a little something different.

I talked to Herbert about it, and he told me that I had stayed at his church for several years, so now he would join my church. I was so thankful for such an understanding man! And that is exactly what he did. He joined my church and became a member of the senior choir as well as the male chorus.

Desmond attended Sunday school, was in the Tots' choir, and became one of the children's ushers when he got a little older.

Herbert was a doting father to both of the boys. He loved them as if they were ours by birth, and so did I. When the boys were younger, Saturdays became their day to hang out with their Daddy. He loved to take them fishing out on the boat with his Uncle or fishing on the pier.

That was a weekly thing during the spring and summer. And they all so looked forward to it. Life was great for a while, and then we began to face some challenges.

We continued our lives and raising our children for several years. We participated in a lot of family gatherings, holidays, cookouts, and different events. On one such occasion on July 4, 1996, while at a cookout at my sister's house, our lives changed forever. We were sitting in the living room, enjoying our food, when my niece noticed that Herbert had an odd look on his face. He was saying something, but his speech was slurred. Someone else said he's just joking as he always does.

However, I noticed that there was something different about this time. It was not his normal joking nature. His speech was slurred, and my sister, a registered nurse, said someone needed to call 911, which we did immediately. Paramedics came, and Herbert was transported to the hospital. Upon my arrival there, I was told that he had a stroke. It was quite a shock, and I prayed to God to strengthen me. Joshua 1:9 says:

> "Have not I commanded thee? Be strong and of a good courage; be not afraid, neither be thou dismayed: for the LORD thy God is with thee whithersoever thou goest."

The stroke affected his left side, and he was unable to speak clearly. Initially, he was unable to walk or use his left side at all. Thank God the call had been made soon enough to paramedics that they could assess the situation quickly enough, that it hadn't gotten any more severe. Following his stroke, a treatment plan was put in place.

Subsequently, Herbert was hospitalized for a couple of weeks, followed by an aggressive physical therapy plan. He remained in a rehabilitation center for a couple of months before he was released to come home.

Although Herbert was able to walk again with an assistive device, he had limited use of his left hand. With extensive speech therapy, his speech came back to him, and he could be understood clearly. God is so good! Psalms 124:8 says:

> "Our help is in the name of the LORD, who made heaven and earth."

I was so thankful that he came through that and still had a reasonable portion of health and strength. He was not bedridden and could still get around. That was a blessing.

However, he was no longer able to work. That was okay. He had survived the stroke, and that was what was important.

This was now a new season in our lives. Our "new normal," if you will. With this new normal came financial difficulties. We applied for disability for him, but it did not get approved right away. With only my income coming in, bills began to fall behind. The savings that we had was quickly depleted.

Herbert had purchased a house on his GI Bill when he came out of the military, so we were able to live there for a while, but it soon became too much to handle. We previously had some remodeling done, and that coupled with routine repairs to keep the house up and running became overwhelming.

Because he worked with his hands, Herbert had been able to do many repairs himself before the stroke, but he was no longer able to do that. Things had been going well as long as we were both working, but when our circumstances changed, I began looking for somewhere for us to rent.

All of this was in God's plan. Do you want to know how I know? Because he already had a place picked out for us. As I was skimming through the newspaper one day, a description of a house caught my eye. I wanted to stay in the city of Norfolk, and I wanted to be in a school district that I was familiar with. I called the phone number associated with the listing and spoke with a genuinely nice lady who told me that the house was available and asked if I could come and meet with her in a day or two. I told her yes, by all means.

A few days later, Herbert, Tyler (our second son), who was five years old, and I got in the car and went to the appointment to see the house. It was just what we needed. Two bedrooms and a bathroom all on one level because it was difficult for Herbert to manipulate steps.

We did not need anything large. It also included a washer and dryer, and it was a price range that we could afford.

The landlord also lived in the neighborhood. After touring the house, she took us to her house to fill out an application and discuss the details. She seemed to be a very nice lady. She was older and seemed to be very impressed with us. She was also amazed at Tyler's behavior, only being five years old. She told me that many other potential tenants (because she owned several houses) had brought children with them, and they would run all through the house, pick up things, wouldn't sit down, and did not know how to act.

I told her, "Oh no, rest assured Tyler knows how to behave." I also let her know that she did not have to worry about him tearing up her property if she rented to us. She was amazed at how well behaved he was, as he just sat on the sofa where I told him to sit and did not try to get up or wander around, but simply played with his toy. He quietly sat while we took care of business. That is the way that we raised our children. They knew how to act appropriately. Thank you, Lord, for obedient children.

I filled out the application, discussed the details, and then left. A few days later, we received a call saying that we were approved. To let you know how good God is, we moved on December 1, 2000, and lived there until I moved out on March 31, 2016. That was our home for 16 years. I know that God had that place for us. Philippians chapter 4:19 says:

> "But my God shall supply all your needs according to his riches in glory by Christ Jesus."

Thank you, Lord, for being Jehovah, Jireh, my provider!

She was an awesome landlord. In 16 years, she only raised our rent one time. If ever I called her because something needed to be repaired, she would send someone that day or no later than the very next day. She believed in keeping her properties up. God knew that I needed someone that would be dependable because I was trying to care for a sick husband, still work full time, and raise a small child. Look at God!

After moving, things seemed to be going well. Herbert had gotten a little bit better as far as his mobility and his thought processes. I decided to take a part-time job to go along with my full-time job. Still, in my desired field, I took a job at a group home in Virginia Beach. By now, I had made team leader at my job at Southeastern, so my hours were 8 to 5 or 9 to 6. I was able to get hours at the group home from 6 am until 8:30 am to get the clients up and ready to catch their transportation to their jobs.

I was able to work for two to three additional hours in the morning. There were also a couple of evenings that they needed me if one of the other staff could not come in. If I left

Southeastern around 5 pm, I would be there until about 7 pm. I had no babysitting issues because Herbert's cousin kept Tyler for me during my extra work hours.

I worked on this schedule for about two months before I began to notice something about my husband. His light had gone out. He was no longer as happy-go-lucky as he had been even after the stroke. He had begun to show signs of depression, which was not okay with me.

I decided on two things. First and foremost, I was going to quit my part-time job. No amount of money was worth my husband's unhappiness.

Secondly, I was going to find a day program for him to participate in. He was spending entirely too much time alone. That thought had never crossed my mind because I didn't see any outward signs at first. He seemed to be doing okay during the day with watching television, talking to his friends on the phone, having visitors, etc.

I would leave his breakfast prepared in the microwave, so it was just a matter of heating it. I would also always leave his lunch in the refrigerator, something simple he could eat like a sandwich or salad and fruit. And it had been working well, or so I thought.

After a time, I noticed a difference, and I asked him about it. He was truthful and told me that he did sometimes get terribly lonely during the day. I felt so guilty and so bad that I did not see this coming. I asked my husband to please forgive me because I would never knowingly put him in a position of unhappiness. Of course, he was very understanding and told me that he knew that I was trying to do my best to help the family by taking on a second job, but I promised him that I would never do that again!

I prayed and asked God to please help me to find the appropriate placement for him while I was at work. Psalms 46 verse 1 says:

> "God is our refuge and strength, a very present help in trouble."

As He always does, God answered my prayer. I found an adult daycare center where I could drop Herbert off in the mornings on my way to work and pick him up in the evenings on my way home. That way, he had socialization all day long while I was at work and no longer had to be alone. Thank you, Lord, once again for working things out.

This went on for about a year-and-a-half. After a time, I noticed that Herbert seemed to be slowing down a bit. I took him to the doctor to discover that another problem had developed. Herbert had begun to have issues with his heart.

He was diagnosed with something called cardiomyopathy, which is a stretching of the heart muscles. It is a weakening of the heart muscles, and there was no way to get the elasticity back. It manifests through shortness of breath, retaining fluid, and congestive heart failure. Ultimately, it was determined that the probable cause of this was his active duty in the Vietnam War and exposure to Agent Orange.

Herbert's condition worsened. He had a few mini-strokes and heart-related hospitalizations that followed. After a while, the doctor told me that his heart was only functioning at ten percent and that the prognosis was not good. I was told that he could pass away because his heart could give out at any moment. I was given this report in 1999.

My prayer was, "God, I know that you are a keeper. I also know that the doctors do not have the final say, that only you have the final say, dear Lord." My faith remained strong, my trust and belief were strong, and I knew God would sustain us.

Let me just tell you about the God that I serve! My husband did not pass away in 1999, 2000, or 2001. I continued to take him to church, family gatherings, and other activities we participated in as long as he felt up to it.

If something was going on and he did not want to go, I stayed home with him. I did not mind this at all. I enjoyed the time that we were able to spend together. If we stayed home, one of my family members would always come and pick up Tyler and take him to whatever the activity was, so he never missed out on anything. When we did go somewhere, my family knew and understood his limitations. I would tell them, "You all go on ahead, and we will get there eventually." They would take Tyler and go on, and I would stay with Herbert, allowing him to take his time ambulating, stopping to rest, or whatever he needed.

I had once suggested a wheelchair when we were going out, but he told me that he wanted to be independent just as long as he could. And I understood and appreciated it as well. I think that is one of the reasons that he lasted longer than the doctors expected because God gave him the will to keep living!

At the beginning of 2002, I noticed that he was slowing down quite a bit and began using a wheelchair. He could no longer attend the adult daycare because he was not what they considered independent enough anymore. He was able to continue there through June.

I was told that I would have to find other placement for him because it was too risky to continue allowing him there. My heart was broken.

He definitely could not be at home while I was working. What was I to do? I had to work. I was still raising a child who was seven years old at that time.

My prayer this time was, "God, please help me, show me what to do." I prayed about the situation, and God gave me my answer. A few days, I had to leave Herbert home for a couple of hours while I ran errands. Over two weeks, there were two instances that this occurred, so I knew what I had to do.

Leaving him alone even that small amount of time had become a safety issue. On those two occasions, I came home, and Herbert was lying on the floor. He had fallen and could not get himself up. This was not good, and I knew this could not continue. Proverbs 3:5-6 says:

"Trust in the LORD with all thine heart; and lean not unto thine own understanding. In all thy ways acknowledge him, and he shall direct thy paths."

Regretfully, I started researching nursing facilities. I knew something about nursing facilities because my Daddy had been in one. I researched several places and decided on Sentara Newtown Road in Virginia Beach, Virginia. It had excellent ratings and was relatively new at that time.

I took Herbert and a couple of family members and visited the facility. We were pleased with what we saw and heard and knew that we would have to make it a priority to be there to keep a check on things.

The facility was only about a ten-minute drive from where I worked, making it easy access for me to stop in at different times of the day. I promised Herbert that I would be there every day.

As time went by, I saw that he was getting slower and weaker. He was admitted to the nursing facility in the first part of July. It was already difficult knowing that was what I had to do, but it was even harder because it was right around the time of our 20th wedding anniversary, which was July 3rd. My heart was broken having to leave my husband there. We had always been inseparable and did everything together. I kept my promise, though.

Visiting became a part of my daily routine. Some days I would stop on my way to work to check on him, and, sometimes, I would check on him on my lunch break. There were other times that I would stop in twice a day, sometimes before and after work, sometimes at lunch, and after work. Sometimes I stopped before work, and at lunch, so they knew that I would be there daily. They also knew that my sisters, my brother, nieces, nephews, and Herbert's brother and sister-in-law, who were both doctors, would also be coming. I must say that I was not disappointed at all. He was very well taken care of.

Herbert passed away on September 9, 2002. This was three years past the time that the doctors had given him. Revelation 21:4 says:

> "And God shall wipe away all tears from their eyes; and there shall be no more death, neither sorrow, nor crying, neither shall there be any more pain: for the former things are passed away."

Herbert was now at peace. I could not have asked for a better husband or father to our children. God allowed us 20 wonderful years together, and for that, I was grateful! I love and miss you, Herbert, my one and only true love. My gentle giant.

Walking by faith while becoming parents

My husband Herbert and I were blessed with a number of children in our lives. Two became permanent parts of our home and our children.

One day, in early February 1987, we received a phone call informing us that a young woman had a child that she wanted to put up for adoption. She had four other children. At only 25 years old, she could not afford to take care of another child. It was a little boy, and she wanted him to go to a home that was full of love, care and to a couple who would be able to provide a decent life for him.

We had been married for five years at that time and hadn't had a child of our own. We had never really discussed adoption, and we weren't pressed to have children. We were just taking life as it came. We prayed and talked about what it would entail.

The next morning, we decided to go to the hospital where the child was, meet the mother, and see how things went. Matthew 7:7-8 says:

> "Ask, and it shall be given you; seek, and ye shall find; knock, and it shall be opened unto you. For everyone that asketh, receiveth; and he that seeketh, findeth; and to him that knocketh, it shall be opened."

Our prayer was, "Lord, we are asking and seeking your will for this decision in our lives. You have given us this opportunity for a reason; show us what to do with it, Lord."

Arriving at the hospital, we met a beautiful young lady who said that she could not take care of this child. She wanted the child to go to a loving home and had asked for recommendations. Our name was provided to her as a couple who might be interested and had no children of their own yet.

We were informed that the child would have to leave the hospital in the next couple of days because he was healthy, and there was no reason for him to stay once the mother was discharged. We were led to the nursery, where we laid eyes upon the most beautiful little curly-head baby boy that you would ever want to see. Of course, we immediately fell in love.

We agreed to take the baby with the understanding that we would obtain a lawyer for a private, legal adoption. We also made the stipulation that once the child left the hospital and was legally adopted, the birth mother or father would no longer have contact with the child until the child became 18 and if he so desired.

We wanted it understood that if we agreed to adopt this child, he would be our child and raised with our morals and standards. We did not want contact, visitation, or any of that while the child was under the legal age. We also explained to the birth mother that we would explain that he was adopted when we felt that the child was old enough to understand.

We would, however, explain that his birth mother loved him but was unable to care for him. She wanted what was best for him and wanted him to go to a family that could provide for him to live a comfortable and loving life.

The birth mother told us that we would have the honor of naming him whatever we wanted. It was arranged for us to pick the baby up the next day.

Herbert and I left the hospital excited, thanking God for this unexpected blessing. We immediately got in the car and prayed, giving thanks to God. We asked for His guidance and for him to show us if we were doing the right thing.

We then went to do some baby shopping. We purchased a car seat, clothes, a bassinet, a few toys, a teddy bear, the kind of formula that they told us that he was on at the hospital, and, of course, diapers. We discussed names. We were so excited at this unexpected blessing. We both agreed on the name Desmond Andrew Stiff.

When we got home, we consulted a lawyer who specialized in private adoptions and explained our situation. He arranged for us to come in and see him the very next morning before we went to pick the baby up. He explained all the adoption would entail and informed us that we would have to put a notice of publication in the newspaper to give the father a chance to come forward if he were interested in claiming the child.

This publication had to run for a couple of months to give the father ample time to see it in the newspaper. The name that would be used to identify the child was baby boy and the birth mother's last name. That would be the indicator to the father who the baby was if he had not been informed of the pregnancy.

We proceeded to get the ball rolling because we wanted the adoption to be completed as soon as possible. Colossians 3:17 says:

> "And whatsoever ye do in word or deed, do all in the name of the Lord Jesus, giving thanks to God and the Father by him."

We were so grateful. "Lord, we thank you for the opportunity of changing a child's life as well as enriching our own!"

We picked Desmond up from the hospital after leaving the lawyer's office. That day was his one-week-old birthday. We had not told any of our family members about our surprise, so on the way home, we stopped at my mother and father's house,

Herbert's mom's house, and his older cousins Cindy and Joe's house.

They were all so surprised, happy, as well as shocked. And, just like us, they immediately fell in love. I then called my sisters and brothers and told them about the baby, and they were so excited for us. Those that lived in Norfolk came by to see him in the next day or two.

My brother and sister-in-law, who lived in New York, were also overjoyed and planned to see us soon. As Herbert and I were both still working full time, we needed someone to keep the baby.

Cousin Cindy volunteered for that job. She ran a home daycare and only had a couple of other children there. That was a blessing because I knew my child would be safe and in good hands. God was putting everything right into place. It was all falling in line with his will for us. 1 Chronicles 16:11 says:

> "Seek the LORD and his strength, seek his face continually."

We would definitely be seeking the Lord and His strength continually for this new season in our lives. Thank you, Lord!

I took six weeks of maternity leave from work so that the baby would be almost two months when I went back to work. Herbert took off two weeks so that we both could be home and bond with Desmond. It was a beautiful, happy, and enjoyable time for the three of us, getting to know each other.

Everything went smoothly, and the adoption was completed right around his first birthday.

The father never answered the newspaper publication, so things moved forward from there. To God be the glory. No problems, no glitches, just smooth sailing. That let us know that God ordained it. He had given us His answer.

Desmond was already potty-trained by the age of two, so we enrolled him in Greenhill Farms Christian Academy. He was a very bright child, and he thrived at that school. He was also a member of the Tots' choir at church and the children's usher board. He was a loving, happy-go-lucky child. He loved going to school and church.

Desmond turned six years old on February 5, 1993. Things were going very well until one day, mid-February 1993, I received a call that Desmond was sick at school and needed to be picked up. I began praying right then.

I went to Greenhill Farms and picked him up, and they said he had been throwing up. He did not have a fever or anything, so I took him home and put him to bed so that he could rest. We had been home for an hour or two before he began to have diarrhea and vomiting.

I told Herbert what was going on when he got home from work. It was now after hours, so I called the emergency line to the doctor's office because he developed a fever and blood was in his stool. They told us to take him immediately to the Children's Hospital of the King's Daughters.

Naturally, we were praying the whole time for God to heal our child. When we got him to the hospital, they immediately took him to the back to be evaluated because they saw how sick he was. He was constantly throwing up, and his diarrhea had turned to pure blood.

Desmond even asked me, "Mommy, am I going to die?" That was how sick our little boy was.

Herbert and I were very concerned. Our hearts were breaking, wishing that we could take the sickness, take the pain and discomfort, instead of him. After all, he was just a sweet innocent child suffering like he was.

We called Herbert's brother and sister-in-law, who lived in Hampton and were both physicians. My sister-in-law was a pediatrician who often sent patients to King's Daughters and was on staff there. I also called my family members as well as Desmond's godparents. We were all praying so hard because we did not know what was going on.

When my sister-in-law got to the hospital, she immediately consulted with the ER physicians. Desmond had already been admitted and put in ICU. We were told that he was very, very, sick and they would be doing tests to see the cause of the problem. Naturally, Herbert and I were not leaving that hospital, so we spent a few nights there.

They made Desmond as comfortable as they could by putting him in a coma. After about two days of testing, my sister-in-law and the doctor came to talk to us about what they had found. Before coming up with a diagnosis, they had us do food diaries for two weeks of meals to see what he had eaten and if any of the other children eating the same thing had gotten sick or had any of his symptoms.

He had spent the weekend with a friend of his, and no one in that household had gotten ill, nor had Herbert or me, nor had any of the other children or teachers at school. My sister-in-law and the doctors talked to us and told us that he had Hemolytic Uremic Syndrome, which seemed to be caused by E. coli bacteria. Each of his organs had begun shutting down, one by one, starting with his kidneys, then his lungs, heart, etc.

There was no cure for this and, if he survived, he would be a vegetable and unable to do anything but lie there. This seemed to be so unfair for a sweet, loving, and active six-year-old.

I kept asking the question, "Why God? Why our child? What did he ever do to deserve this?" We were faced with the difficult decision of taking him off life support.

We prayed and asked God to show us what to do. We had been praying for his healing and did not expect this at all. I thought back to when Desmond asked me was he going to die, and I had assured him no. "No, baby, you're at the hospital, and the doctors are going to help you feel better. God is going to heal you." Our faith was strong, and we knew it was true: He was going to be healed. But, sometimes, things turn out differently than we imagine. Psalms 34:15 says:

> "The eyes of the LORD are upon the righteous, and his ears are open unto their cry."

Our baby boy was healed, but he got the ultimate healing. He was healed by God and taken home to be with Him where he would suffer no more.

I must be totally transparent here and admit that Herbert and I were so confused. Things had happened so quickly. All of this happened in a matter of less than one week. Speaking for myself, I was really angry. I did not understand how God could allow this to happen to an innocent child. Psalms 34:15 says:

> "The eyes of the Lord are upon the righteous, and his ears are open unto their cry."

I was seeking the Lord, hoping to find some understanding in this matter.

Desmond's funeral was held at our church. He was in a white casket, trimmed in gold, and had on a white suit. He looked like a little sleeping angel.

The school closed down that day, and everyone there came to the funeral, including parents, teachers, and students. The students dedicated and sang a song to Desmond, and the school's principal had beautiful words to say.

One of the things I will never forget is how the principal said how much Desmond loved us. She said that if we asked him would he rather stay where he was in Heaven or come back down here on Earth to be with us, she was sure he would say that he wanted to stay in the beautiful place where he was. Revelation Chapter 21 gives us a glimpse of Heaven.

> Verse 19 says: "And the foundations of the city were garnished with all manner of precious stones. The first foundation was jasper; the second sapphire; the third, a chalcedony; the fourth, an emerald."

> Verse 21 says: "And the twelve gates were twelve pearls; every several gates was of one pearl: and the streets of the city were pure gold, as it were transparent glass."

> Verse 23 says: "And the city had no need of the sun, neither of the moon, to shine in it; for the glory of God did lighten it, and the Lamb is the light thereof."

I suggest you read the whole chapter for yourself. How in the world could I not want my child to experience this beautiful place? I just wanted him to have more time on Earth with us, his parents who loved him more than life itself.

Herbert and I were broken-hearted. We could hardly function. We both took time off from work. We walked around in a daze, and it felt like if anyone said anything to us, we would lose it!

We hibernated at home for a while, occasionally talking to family and friends who were trying to check on us. We understood their concern, but with an unexpected loss like that, sometimes you just need time to think and process the whole situation without meaning to offend anyone. That was the stage of grief that we were in at that time.

Herbert and I also stayed away from church for a while. I think his reason was more grief than anything. Mine was both grief and anger.

Some may find it bold of me to admit this, but I was angry with God. I thought that we were doing everything right by raising Desmond in a Christian home, sending him to a Christian School, and having him participate in Christian ministries and activities at church. Wasn't that what we were supposed to be doing?

Our staying away from church went on for a couple of months. During that time, it seemed as if I could not even pray. I could not find the words to say.

One night, as I was sleeping, I guess God got tired of my mess because I was awakened abruptly and sat straight up in bed. I heard God say to me very clearly, "I gave my son for you!" That did it! It made things clear to me. Who did I think I was, that my son could not be taken from me when he sacrificed his son on Calvary's Cross for us all, even me?

I want you to know I told my husband what had happened, and he and I prayed and asked God to forgive us. Psalms 86:5 says:

> "For thou, Lord, art good, and ready to forgive; and plenteous in mercy unto all them that call upon thee."

We went back to church the very next Sunday and back to serving in the organizations and ministries that we were a part of. Thank you, God; lesson learned.

It took some time, but our lives got back to some semblance of normalcy. It took us time to get used to the house without the pitter-patter of little feet running to and fro, but we adjusted as best we could.

In 1994, we had two opportunities of bringing children into our home that didn't work out too well. The first opportunity, we were called and told about a newborn baby girl that needed a home. The baby was born drug-addicted. Herbert and I did not think it would be wise for us to take this baby as much as we would love to have had a little girl.

Statistics show that drug-addicted babies sometimes have ongoing problems even in later years of life. After going through what we had been through with Desmond, we didn't think this was a challenge that we could meet. We declined that child and prayed that she would get a loving family capable of handling any deficits that she might have or any special needs that she might have.

The next baby was another little boy. He was born to a 14-year-old girl discharged from the hospital, and her mother would not let her take the baby home. She said that her daughter was too young, and she wanted her to go to school and get her education. Her mother said the baby would be better off being put up for adoption.

Here we go again, I thought. We prayed before we agreed to take the child, although I honestly can't say how much we listened to what God was telling us. We were just so excited at the opportunity to have another child in our home and jumped at the chance.

As previously mentioned, the mother had already been discharged, so it was just a matter of going to pick the baby up, so that's what we did. The mother had already signed papers, which we later found out was at her mother's insistence that she relinquish the baby.

We took the baby home and had him all of 48 hours when we received a phone call. The call said that they were calling on behalf of the baby's birth family. The mother of the 14-year-old had decided that they had to get the baby back. She said all her daughter did was cry. She wouldn't eat nor sleep. She would not do anything but lie in bed and cry.

The 14-year-old's' mother said that she could not let her daughter continue like that, and she should never have demanded that she give the baby up. That was understandable. We were just thankful that we had only had the baby for two days and hadn't even met with the lawyer yet.

We agreed to return the baby. We asked for their address to bring the baby to or if they would prefer to come and pick the baby up from our home. We were told neither. They did not want us to know where their home was, and they preferred not to come to ours.

My question was, "Well, where do you want us to bring the baby?" This is what hurt me more than even having to give the baby back.

The grandmother said, "You know that shopping center called Wards Corner up on Little Creek Road and Granby Street?"

"Yes," I said. "I'm very familiar with it as I shop there often."

She asked, "Do you know where the A&P grocery store is?"

Again, I said, "Yes, I do."

She said, "Well, I will meet you there, and we will pick up the child from there."

I said, "Do you mean in the parking lot by the A&P?"

She said, "Yes."

I was very upset. This poor little innocent child was going to be exchanged in the parking lot in front of the grocery store like a bag of groceries! I had to pray and ask the Lord to give me peace in this matter, as well as to bridle my tongue when I saw this grandmother so that I would not say the wrong thing. I tried to understand that this was a difficult situation for her, but I'm sure we could have made a better decision than exchanging the child in a supermarket parking lot.

That just did not sit well with me, but I asked what time, and she told us the time that she desired. When the time came, Herbert and I put the baby in the car as well as toys and the clothes and diapers and formula that we had purchased, and I took the baby and handed him to his Grandma. She asked if we wanted to be compensated for the items, and we told her no. We just asked that she please love and take care of the sweet little life that was being handed to her.

She thanked us, put the baby in her car, and drove off. As we were riding back home, I prayed for that child. I also knew that child was not meant for us. Needless to say, after those last two incidents, Herbert and I prayed diligently and asked the Lord what He would have us do in regard to children. Time passed, and so did our lives.

Now we come to our second and final child. The one that evidently was truly meant for us. We still had not had a child of our own and had been asking God what He meant for our lives concerning children. Our prayer was, "Lord, if you mean for us to be parents, then lead us to the child that's meant for us. Allow us to know when it is the right one."

On May 13, 1995, we received a phone call about a baby boy that was born to a mother who already had two very young children and was unable to keep this child. We were told that the mother had already signed the paperwork, giving up her rights to the baby. The father would not be an issue at all because he had no interest in the child. She wanted the child to go to a good, loving home that could provide for him.

She did not have to meet the couple that was going to take her child, but she wanted to talk to the prospective mother. I was willing to do that because, in lieu of what happened with the last two attempts at adoption, I needed to speak with her to be assured. She was put on the phone, and I expressed my and my husband's interest in adopting this child. I told her that I could assure her that he would be loved, provided for, and well taken care of.

She, too, wanted to be reassured that he would not be abused or mistreated. I told her that my husband and I absolutely loved children and could never find it in our hearts to hurt a child. I told her that I needed to be reassured that she was certain about her decision because we would be seeking our attorney for a private legal adoption. She said that she thought that would be best and, after that day, we did not have to worry about hearing from her anymore.

She said that she did not want to further confuse her child by being involved in his life. I told her that is what we preferred, but when he turned 18 and needed help, if he wanted to seek her out, we would be willing to do so at his request. I also needed assurance that the father was okay with this. She said that he wanted no involvement with the child.

Well, I knew we would have to go through what we did initially with Desmond and do the publication thing in the newspaper. That was fine with me. After speaking with her on the telephone, she seemed to be satisfied, and we were too. We stopped, prayed, and asked God was He truly giving us the go-ahead for this one. I told Herbert I just kept hearing the words yes, yes, yes in my ears. I truly believed that this was God speaking to me. Isaiah 30:21 says:

> "And thine ears shall hear a word behind thee, saying, this is the way, walk ye in it, when ye turn to the right hand, and when ye turn to the left."

With our faith in tow, we went to the hospital to pick up our new bundle of joy. He was only one day old when we got him. You don't get much newer than that. We hadn't had time to discuss a name or anything. Once again, we surprised everyone with a "drive-by" to meet this new addition to our family. Again, everyone was in shock, awe, and disbelief but was overjoyed for us.

We took the baby home and got him settled in, then began discussing names. After much conversation, we came up with Tyler Kennard Stiff. Thank you, Lord, for our blessing.

When Tyler was exactly one week old, we got a call from the hospital saying that the results of his heel prick test had come in. I asked what the results were. They said that this was the test that determined whether or not your child had sickle cell disease. Tyler's test had come back positive.

We were advised to take him to a pediatrician immediately so that further testing could be done and a plan of action be determined. We would need to be educated on how this condition would affect him. He was supposed to go in for a two-week check-up anyway, so I called and asked if they could see him sooner.

We were informed that he did not have the sickle cell trait but that he had the full-blown disease. This meant that both his mother and father had the sickle cell trait in order for him to be born with the full disease known as Sickle Cell SS.

As soon as we got home, we consulted our sister-in-law, the pediatrician, and she clarified it for us. We were told what to prepare for, how it could manifest itself, and what to watch for.

"Okay, Lord, here we go. Our first child, Desmond, was born healthy with no known disease, then took sick all of a sudden and passed away. But this child, whom we have already fallen in love with, was born with a problem. Yes, we believe that this child is meant for us. Stand by us, Lord. With you, we can do this!"

So, we were in it for the long haul. Our faith was strong, and we believed that the illness was not going to get the best of him and overtake him. This was our prayer, in the name of Jesus:

> "Lord, just give us the strength to endure and do what we have to do. To get him through any crisis that he might have. This is our prayer, in the name of your son Jesus Christ. We count it done."

That prayer did it for us. It said all that we had to say about it, and we were ready to do whatever was required.

The first couple of years of Tyler's life included several hospitalizations, but strangely enough, they were not necessarily due to sickle cell pain crisis but were more respiratory issues. He had several bouts of pneumonia as a baby. He went to the hospital nine times with pneumonia over a period of one year. As he got a little older, we already knew that his immune system was compromised. He was also diagnosed with having asthma, which accounted for so many respiratory issues.

As he grew older, the respiratory issues got better, and he started having more sickle-cell pain crises. His little hands and feet would swell up and be very painful for him to walk or to use his hands. He would have to go into the hospital for treatment. He was also put on specific sickle-cell medications, which prevented him from having as many crises as he would have had without the medication.

Other than that, he was pretty much a normal child, and grew, thrived, and did well. He would get sick and have to be hospitalized every now and then. During some of those hospitalizations, he had to have blood transfusions because his blood count had dropped too low.

Herbert and I never allowed him to be at the hospital alone. As a matter of fact, Herbert would work during the day, and I would take off because I had earned leave on my job. After work, Herbert would go home and rest a bit, then come and join me at the hospital and stay overnight before leaving for work. He was a bricklayer, so he would go to work. After work, he would go home, clean up and rest for a little bit before returning to the hospital.

I tried to get him to stay home some nights because he had a hard job, but because of what had happened to Desmond, he refused to leave Tyler unless he had to. I truly understood the way he felt.

This went on for several years. It just became part of our routine. The doctors were amused because when Tyler went to the doctors, even at four years old, when they asked him what medicines he was on, he could name them by their correct names like he was a doctor or nurse. He was a very bright child, and his medical team was quite impressed.

Tyler grew up as a normal child. He also attended Greenhill Farms Christian Academy, just as Desmond had. He did well in school and never let his illness hold him back. We instilled this in him from a young child. We wanted him to know that yes, sometimes you may have illnesses or other trials and tribulations, but try to never let them get you down.

We wanted him to know that God was always with him and that God would take care of him. Psalms 6:2 says:

> "Have mercy upon me, O LORD; for I am weak: O LORD, heal me; for my bones are vexed."

That being said, he grew up participating in several different sports. He took karate and hip hop dance. He was on the community basketball team, and he performed with a gospel dance group called Honey in the Rock.

He also took acting classes, so he had quite a busy life in spite of his illness. He also was the Sunday school church secretary, sang in the youth choir, was a youth usher, and quite often the Master of Ceremonies on youth Sundays.

Tyler also read the announcements and welcomed the visitors on Sunday mornings. He did well in school. At the end of his high school years, he participated in a program sponsored by Zeta Phi Beta Sorority of Norfolk State University called Men of Tomorrow.

The young people were taught proper etiquette, and they learned how to appropriately escort a young lady, dance a waltz as well as display their public speaking skills by giving a speech that they wrote. He did extremely well and even won second place, which was a large trophy as well as a financial scholarship to the college of his choice. He finished high school and attended Virginia State University.

Throughout his tenure at Virginia State, Tyler was hospitalized about once each semester, with stays usually lasting anywhere from four to seven days. Naturally, these were periods of frustration for him, and he had thoughts of quitting school. Yet, he did not give in and pressed on in spite of the difficulties of being sick.

He sometimes fell behind in his classwork and had to play catch-up, as well as keep the professors advised of what was going on, but he never gave up. I am proud to say that on December 14, 2019, Tyler graduated from Virginia State University with a degree in mass communications. To God be the glory! Ecclesiastes 9:11 says:

> "I returned, and saw under the sun, that the race is not to the swift, nor the battle to the strong, neither yet bread to the wise, nor yet riches to men of understanding, not yet favour to men of skill; but time and chance happeneth to them all."

I often reminded him of how God had kept us. He had kept him even throughout his illness. He had kept him throughout losing his father at a young age, and he had provided all of our needs as the years progressed. God is so faithful! Thank you, Lord!

Walking by faith through a "new normal"

To say the least, life as a widow and as a single mother was challenging. This period in my life really became a "faith walk" for me. John 14:18 says:

"I will not leave you comfortless: I will come to you."

Things that often seemed routine were somewhat different. I still had not fully gotten used to the idea of Herbert no longer being in the house anymore because he went into the nursing home in July, and it was just September when he passed.

I was still trying to get used to the things that he used to do around the house when he was well. Simple things such as pulling the trash can out to the curb, climbing a ladder to put in a lightbulb, fixing things that were broken around the house, and even taking the car to the gas station to fill it up were things Herbert always took care of. Those were things that he always did, and I didn't have to worry about.

It was also very difficult returning to work. I had been on my job for 22 years at that point, was a supervisor, and was pretty well-known at Southeastern Virginia Training Center. I was so grateful to my supervisor, coworkers, the administrative staff, and the staff in every department there for the love and generosity they showed towards me.

We had a program called Leave Share where anyone that wanted to donate some of their leave hours to a staff person could do so. That would enable the person to continue to get paid while they were on leave. Everyone was so very generous in donating leave to me that I was able to stay out a full two months at home with pay. What was so ironic about this was that they had done the exact same thing for me when my son passed a few years before. When he passed, I was able to stay out for three months. Luke 6: 31 says:

> "And as ye would that men should do to you, do ye also to them likewise."

Thank you, Lord, for the love, support, empathy, and sympathy shown to me by my co-workers. It still makes my heart full to know that so many people cared about me!

God always provides what you need when you need it. I truly believe that. I was so drained mentally, emotionally, and physically. God knew that I needed time to rest.

When I returned to work, some days were easier than others. There were days when I would walk into my building, and people would say, "Good morning, how are you doing?" I would respond that I was okay.

Then there were other days when they would ask me, and I would have to hold it together long enough to go into my office and close the door before the tears began to flow. There were days that I had meetings to attend, where I dreaded seeing people that I didn't see on a daily basis because I knew that they would ask me how I was doing. I knew they meant no harm and were only showing concern, but that could be so difficult.

My best friend was a supervisor in the building across the street from me, and I would call her when I was getting ready to go to check my mail in one of the administrative office buildings. I would ask her to please meet me at the door so that I didn't have to go in and walk through the building by myself. We were each other's support system because two years prior to Herbert's passing, her husband had also passed, and she had done the same thing, so she knew exactly what I was feeling. She and her husband were our children's godparents.

God put her and her husband in my life for a reason. I had already been working at Southeastern for a couple of years before she began working there. When I met her, our personalities immediately clicked. As time went on, we became good friends.

Our lives ended up being similar in many ways. When we met, we were both supervisors of our individual shifts. Later, we were both promoted to supervisors of our buildings we referred to as cottages. That is where the residents lived.

Our lives paralleled a lot, and we have always been there for each other throughout the good and difficult times. Thank you, Lord, for my true sister/friend. Matthew 22:39 says:

> "And the second (commandment) is like unto it, Thou shalt love thy neighbor as thyself."

There were some days that I went to work, and I felt okay. Some days I could only make it through half of the day, and I would have to leave. However, as time went on, things got much better.

My main concern was keeping it together for my son Tyler. He and his Dad had been extremely close. He was very sad at first and would not sleep in his room alone for a while, which was understandable. He knew that his Dad was in a beautiful place called Heaven because we've always raised our children in church. He knew that his Dad would still be watching over us and would always love us.

I enrolled Tyler in counseling with a psychologist for a few months so that he could express his feelings about his Daddy's death. I just wanted to be certain that he would be okay.

Children are pretty resilient. As time went on, Tyler was fine. I kept him busy with extracurricular as well as church activities. That helped me also because it helped occupy my mind and time.

One thing that I have learned through all of the loss in my life is that no one can tell you how you should grieve. Everyone grieves differently. I have grieved in several different ways, depending on whom I was grieving for. I grieved differently for my child that passed than I did for my husband. And I grieved differently for my Mom and Dad and other people that I've lost in my life.

One thing that I do know is that God is a comforter. He gives us "a peace that surpasses all understanding," and He "will never leave us, or forsake us." I am a witness to that fact. Philippians 4:7 says:

> "And the peace of God that passes all understanding, shall keep your hearts and minds through Christ Jesus."

Thank you, Lord, for your peace!

One of the main "new normal" things was getting through the first year of holidays and other celebratory days without Herbert. He died in September, so the first major holiday was Thanksgiving. Typically, what we had done ever since we had been married, was split our holidays between our two families.

Sometimes we would go to his family's house for holidays, and other times we'd be with my family. That year, we were with my family for Thanksgiving, which was very difficult because, at all family gatherings, Herbert had always been the life of the party, being funny and telling jokes. Still, we made it.

Christmas that year was also very difficult. We had a tradition with the Stiff family that every Christmas Eve night, we went over to their home and attended church with them. After that, we would go back to their house, and everyone would open one Christmas gift. That Christmas Eve was bittersweet for us all.

However, by the grace of God, we made it! Lord, I thank you for being our comforter during these times.

On New Year's Eve, we always went to church and brought in the New Year on our knees, giving thanks for the blessings of seeing a new year. Going to church and fellowshipping with our church family was extremely comforting to us.

Herbert's birthday, Tyler's birthday, and my birthday were also different that year. Ordinarily, we would go out to dinner and then have the family over to the house to celebrate with ice cream and cake. We always took Tyler to Chuck-E-Cheese or somewhere like that for his birthday, so that tradition did not change except his Dad was not there. We still had the family over to celebrate, but our main jokester was missing.

Tyler and I started new traditions for some things, and as time passed, things got easier. God continued to keep us through his grace and mercy. Once again, my faith has helped me through another major change in my life. Deuteronomy 31: 6 says:

> "Be strong and of a good courage, fear not, nor be afraid of them: for the LORD thy God, he it is that doth go with thee; he will not fail thee, nor forsake thee."

Thank you, Lord, for being with me during this new time in my life, and thank you for your faithfulness to me. Indeed, great is your faithfulness and each day new mercies I see. You have faithfully provided all that I have needed.

Walking by faith during the onset of illnesses

During this time in my faith walk, I had adjusted well to being back to work and getting on with life. Often on my lunch break, I would go into the stores and look around. I had an hour break, so that gave me time to do a little shopping if I wanted to.

One day, I was in Burlington in the housewares department, looking around. The next thing I knew, I woke up lying flat on my back on the floor.

Looking up, I saw several people standing over me, and someone was shaking me, asking was I okay. Evidently, while pushing my cart, I had blacked out.

I began to try to explain that I was diabetic and that my blood sugar must have dropped. I had been diagnosed with Type 2 diabetes several years prior and was taking medication, so it had not been a problem. I had never had this happen to me before because it seemed to be controlled with the medication that I was taking.

When I woke up, my speech was slurred, and it was difficult to understand me. Finally, someone understood and said, "Oh, you're diabetic." I said yes. Someone who was standing there had candy in their purse and gave it to me to put in my mouth. This was something new and different for me, passing out like this. 911 was called, and I was transported to the emergency room.

In the ambulance, I was given glucose to bring my blood sugar up because it was still too low when they checked it. I also called my supervisor to tell her what had happened and called my sister as well. After being monitored at the emergency room for a while, my sister came to pick me up and took me home.

Before leaving, I was told that I needed to purchase some glucose tablets to keep in my purse at all times, to take when I felt like my sugar was dropping. On the way home, my sister stopped at the drug store to get the tablets for me. I went home, ate something, and laid down.

My sister picked up my son and took him to her house, telling me that she would get him to school the next day. I returned to work the next day, and everything was fine. Thank you, Lord! Isaiah 41:10 says:

> "Fear thou not; for I am with thee: be not dismayed; for I am thy God: I will strengthen thee; yea, I will help thee;

yea, I will uphold thee with the right hand of my righteousness."

About two months later, I specifically remember it was in the month of May because I had been to Party City to purchase balloons for my son's birthday. On the way home, I blacked out behind the wheel of my car and ended up in someone's front yard. Thank God for His mercy and grace. I was not injured, nor was anyone else. I didn't even hit anything and somehow was able to put the car in park. Psalms 121:8 says:

"The LORD shall preserve thy going out and thy coming in from this time forth, and even for evermore."

Lord, thank you for your protection. People came running out of the house, and I remember being very groggy and confused. They were asking me if I was okay, and my speech was again slurred. I told them that my blood sugar must be too low. Some of them probably thought that I was drunk because if it were me seeing the same situation, I might have thought the same thing listening to the person speak.

I remember someone running into a house and coming back out with a peanut butter and jelly sandwich, telling me to eat it. In the meantime, they asked was there anyone that they could call for me. I was able to give them my sister's phone number, and 911 was called.

Several people stayed with me until my sister arrived. Both she and the ambulance arrived at the same time. I ate the sandwich and also took some of my glucose tablets. When the paramedics got there and checked me out, my blood sugar had returned to where it needed to be. They did not have to transport me to the emergency room this time, thank God!

My sister had brought her husband along, so I got in the car with her. She was a registered nurse so she could monitor me. Her husband got in my car and drove it home as she drove me home in hers.

Before leaving, she sent her husband across the street to get me a soda that had sugar in it. She wanted me to drink that to make sure that my blood sugar stayed stable. I felt much better once I got home and laid down. They picked Tyler up from the babysitter and took him home with them overnight. They told me that they would meet me at Chuck E. Cheese the next day, where his party was going to be held.

When this happened, I had my glucose tablets in my pocketbook, so I did not feel my blood sugar dropping as I was driving. My blood sugar had dropped all of a sudden. Anyway, I am thankful that everything was fine after that, and the next day I was able to pick up the cake feeling just fine. With cake and balloons in tow, I went to the party, and everything went well. Tyler, his cousins, and friends had a ball! Lord, I thank you for allowing me to feel well enough so that my baby's party was not ruined.

After this incident, I went to the doctor. There, they did blood work and adjusted my medication. When I went back to the doctor for a follow-up visit, I was told that my blood work showed that my kidney function numbers, specifically my bun and creatinine levels, were not where they should be. I was told that this would have to be closely monitored because this indicated possible kidney issues.

After that, everything was fine for a while. I went to all of my follow-up appointments as scheduled and was being closely monitored. One day, in 2003, while working at my desk, I noticed what appeared to be little black spots moving in front of my eyes. They almost looked like little gnats flying in front of me.

I kept trying to swat at them and blink my eyes, but it did no good. I didn't pay it much attention that day. I just figured my eyes must be tired because I had been working on the computer a lot that day. I finished my workday and went home. I noticed while driving home that the same thing was happening with my eyes. I went to bed early that night to try to give my eyes a rest.

When I woke up the next morning, I still had these spots in front of my eyes. I prepared for work, but as soon as my eye doctor's office opened, I called to express my concern about what was going on and to see if I could get an appointment for some time that day. They were able to see me in the early afternoon. I took half of the day off so that I could go to the appointment.

When I got to the doctor, and she examined my eyes, she told me that I had a detached retina. I asked her how that could have happened. My eye doctor explained that sometimes people who are diabetics have this problem. She immediately referred me to a retina specialist.

Her nurse was able to get me to see a retina specialist whom she recommended that same afternoon because this was an emergency situation that needed to be handled and treated right away.

Treatment for this condition at the time was supposed to be positioning. I was supposed to be in a downward-facing position for at least a week. This was supposed to allow the retina to reattach itself.

Of course, that would require me to take time off from work. With my particular job, I certainly could not be in a downward position. However, the positioning only lasted for two days. It was very difficult to accomplish. And, after the second day, I ended up in the hospital. Of all times, my kidney disease had gotten to the point that I could no longer wait and would have to start dialysis very soon.

I was in the hospital so that they could install a fistula in my arm because it needed time to mature before they could use it for dialysis. However, in order to start immediately, they put a catheter in my chest. I was told that within the next couple of weeks to a month, I would have to start dialysis treatments. Ecclesiastes 3:1 says:

> "To everything there is a season, and a time to every purpose under the heaven."

So now I realized that I was entering a new season. "Okay, Lord, by faith, I'm going with you as my guide."

As soon as I came out of the hospital, I had to go back to the eye doctor to try to get that issue under control. A temporary remedy had been done to my eye until I could come out of the hospital.

The doctor scheduled surgery on my eye to insert oil and a band to hold the retina in place temporarily until I could get the dialysis treatment underway.

This was so hard, as it seemed as if everything was hitting me at once. Still, I knew that God was in control. Exodus 14:14 says:

> "The LORD shall fight for you, and ye shall hold your peace."

I scheduled an appointment at the dialysis center for a tour and to speak with the director and the social worker. My sisters went with me, and everything was explained to us. It was also explained that I would check back into the hospital for my initial treatment because they needed to watch me and make sure that everything was working well with the catheter because they wouldn't be able to use my arm for a couple of months. That's about how long it would take it to mature.

I was a bit apprehensive about starting dialysis, but I was also thankful that I was familiar with it because my Mama had been on it. At the time my treatments began, my oldest sister was also on dialysis at the same treatment center that I would be going to. Her treatment days were Tuesday, Thursday, and Saturday, and mine would be Monday, Wednesday, and Friday.

A couple of weeks went by before I checked into the hospital and had my initial dialysis treatment. Ironically, the date was September 23rd, the day before my birthday. Happy birthday to me!

Still, I looked at it as a blessing because anyone who knows anything about dialysis knows that once you get to end-stage renal disease if you do not take dialysis, you will not live long.

If your kidneys are no longer functioning properly, they cannot filter out the impurities and poisons in your system. Without either dialysis or a kidney transplant, these toxins can back up in your body, and they can/will kill you.

My philosophy in life has always been to try to see the positive aspect of things. I am a "glass-half-full" person as opposed to a "glass is half empty" person. It is so much better to see the positive side of things as opposed to the negative. As such, my motto has always been "positive vibes only."

My first treatment went well, and they kept me two more days so I could do a second treatment while there. I was then allowed to go home.

My third treatment was done at the dialysis center. I got used to going to the dialysis center and having my treatments. In a couple of months, they were able to take the catheter out of my chest and began using my arm. That required being stuck with two needles in my arm each time I went for treatment.

The needles held tubing, which allowed the blood to circulate through the tubing into the dialysis machine, which would clean the blood and then return the blood back into my body. This has to be done three times a week, either for the rest of my life or until I find a donor match and can get a kidney transplant.

Throughout this process, I was forced to learn patience. I am currently on the transplant list, but right now, my status is inactive due to another medical issue that was discovered.

You cannot have anything else wrong with you in order to be a viable candidate for a transplant. I also have another condition with my lungs called pulmonary hypertension, for which I am on medication. Until that gets resolved, I cannot be active on the transplant list.

I know that everything is going to work out for my good; I just have to be patient. After all, it is not in my time but in God's time. In the meantime, I had to go on short-term disability from my job. But it was okay because I was still getting paid while receiving these life-sustaining treatments. For this, I am thankful. Romans 8:28 says:

> "And we know that all things work together for good to them that love God, to them who are the called according to his purpose."

As time passed, I had to have two more surgeries on my left eye. The vision could not be fully corrected, but that was okay.

I can still see out of my right eye and have limited vision in the left eye. Thank you, Lord, for the vision that I have.

Then, on one non-dialysis day in July 2005, I was going to go to the store to pick up a few things. As I attempted to stand up, I immediately fell back down into the chair that I was getting up from. Feeling pain in my left foot, I just assumed that I had been sitting with it in the wrong position, or maybe I had a cramp in it.

I sat there and moved my foot around for a bit, hoping to maybe work the kink out. I then attempted to stand again and again felt the same pain. However, I was able to continue standing and began attempting to walk. I was able to put a little bit of weight on that foot, but not much.

I called my podiatrist, where I was going to get my nails cut, and told him about the problem. He told me that he had an opening that afternoon if I could get there, so I told him that I would be there. Thank God it was my left foot and not my driving foot.

I went to the doctor's office. I told him the issue that I was having and that I did not have an incident of falling, twisting my ankle, hitting my foot, or anything of that nature. I was told that I needed X-rays and that he wanted me to stay off of that foot until the X-ray results were determined.

I explained to him that I needed to go to my dialysis treatment, so he sent me directly from his office to have X-rays done.

Hopefully, the X-ray results could be read immediately, and a plan of action could be determined.

The X-ray results came back showing that I had something called Charcot foot. This is a condition that sometimes occurs in diabetics. What happens is a bone in the foot will deteriorate without you even realizing it until you have the initial onset of pain, and it shows up through an X-ray. You do not have to do anything traumatic to your foot for the bone to break. Because your bones are brittle, they automatically deteriorate from normal wear and tear.

When I went back to the podiatrist, I was told that he did not specialize in this and that I needed to see a podiatrist that could also perform surgery. I was given the name of one of the top foot surgeons in my area at the time. He was an extremely busy man. However, due to the seriousness of my case, I was able to get an appointment within a couple of days.

He determined that surgery was necessary to correct this problem. He would have to go in and install rods in my foot to keep the bone from breaking more, as well as to support me so that I could eventually walk on the foot. Surgery was scheduled. I was told that following the surgery, I would not be able to bear weight on that foot at all.

I would be wheelchair-bound for a few months because a big metal apparatus that held the rods and screws in place would have to be put into my foot, and it had to stay there for several months. It could not be removed except by the doctor, so I even had to sleep in it. It was very uncomfortable and intrusive.

I ended up having to go on long-term disability after being employed by the state for 25 years. I had a three-month hospital stay in the Extended Care Unit of Norfolk General Hospital. I could not stand or bear weight for quite a while in order for the foot to heal correctly.

Disability was very difficult for me because I loved my job. I also loved my residents, some of whom I had worked with for many years, as well as my coworkers.

Another issue was that my home's exterior was not wheelchair accessible. Once I got in there, however, I could move things around so that I would be able to get around in the wheelchair. However, getting up the steps and getting into the house was an issue. But God is so faithful; He always has a ram in the bush.

One of the deacons of my church owns his own construction company. I gave him a call and asked would he be able to construct a temporary ramp for me to be able to get in and out of my home.

I also let him know that I needed it to be done as soon as possible, at least by the time that I got out of the hospital. He was more than willing to accommodate me and did. To God be the glory!

When I got home from the hospital, there was a very nice-looking professionally done ramp leading from the walkway over the stairs so that I could enter and exit the house more easily. Philippians 4:19 says:

> "But my God shall supply all your needs according to his riches in glory by Christ Jesus."

Lord, I thank you for making a way. I used to drive myself to dialysis, but I could no longer do that for the time being. Subsequently, I had to arrange to be transported by medical transport to dialysis. I didn't like that at all because I prided myself on being independent, even with my setbacks. But I knew that it was only temporary.

During that time, my sister, who was next to the oldest, lived within walking distance of me. She was kind enough to volunteer to come and stay with me during the week to help me with Tyler as well as cook, clean, do laundry, and do whatever else was necessary. She was a widow, and her children were grown, so I was thankful that she was willing to do that. My sister, that is one year older than me would come over on the weekends to relieve her.

That sister's husband would be at home with their two boys and, a lot of times, would keep Tyler for the weekend. After several months, the device was removed, and I was able to walk and drive again. Things returned to normal.

Then, in 2009, I began having problems with my stomach. I was experiencing intermittent bouts of pain and discomfort. I was diagnosed with irritable bowel syndrome and was given medication to help control it. It worked for a while. However, after a few months, I started experiencing a different kind of discomfort that became quite painful.

Again, I went to the doctor. They ran tests and discovered that I had gallstones that were very large. I was initially given medicine to try to dissolve them but to no avail. My doctor determined that I needed to have surgery.

I checked into the hospital and had surgery to remove the gallstones as well as my gallbladder. They also ended up removing my appendix. This was due to the fact once they got me in for the surgery, they saw what could potentially be a problem with my appendix, so they felt that it was better to go on and remove it at that same time. I recovered well from that surgery, had no further problems, and felt much relief.

In the month of February 2011, while having my dialysis treatment, I went into cardiac arrest. I had no idea what was happening to me. All I know is that I woke up in the emergency room, and both of my sisters and my brother were standing over me. They told me that I had been transported there by ambulance from the dialysis center because while receiving treatment, I had experienced cardiac arrest. I was told that the nurses had to cut my clothes off of me and use the defibrillator to shock my heart back to functioning. I was totally shocked.

I'd had no prior heart issues or chest discomfort, or anything to indicate a problem. I did not even feel bad during my treatment before it happened.

They ran several tests but couldn't find any heart damage or issues. They did say that dialysis can be hard on the heart, and that was probably what happened. They decided, as a preventative measure, to install a defibrillator in my chest.

I will never forget that on Valentine's Day, February 14, 2011, a defibrillator was installed in my chest. The purpose of the defibrillator installation was to shock my heart back into a normal rhythm if something like that should ever happen again. I was in the hospital for a few days, and then I was released.

Everything was fine for about a year. Then, one afternoon while attempting to get up from a nap, I went to stand up and was knocked back down on the bed. I attempted to get up again and was instantly knocked back down again.

Thank God I kept my cell phone on the table next to my bed as I reached for it and called 911. I did not know what was happening. It felt like someone was kicking me in my chest and knocking me down every time I tried to get up. The paramedics came and said that my heart rate was extremely high, and they gave me some medicine to slow it down and transported me to the emergency room.

When I got to the emergency room, I was checked out and told that my defibrillator was malfunctioning. This was not my regular hospital that had all of my records, and I requested to be transported to that hospital. The powerful sensation that kept knocking me back down on the bed had been the defibrillator going off. And it did not need to as my heart was fine.

They obliged me and took me to my regular hospital, where I was told that I needed to have a procedure to correct the problem with my defibrillator. The procedure was called an ablation. My heart was functioning fine, yet the defibrillator had kicked it out of rhythm by malfunctioning. The ablation procedure would take care of that so it would not occur again. The procedure was performed, and I was kept for observation for a couple of days and sent home. I haven't had any more problems with the defibrillator since.

In September of 2018, a problem occurred with my right foot. I had stopped going to the podiatrist that did my initial foot surgery because the foot had healed so well. That had been a few years prior, and I'd had no problems since then. The only time I needed to go to the podiatrist after that was every three months to have my toenails cut.

Since that was the only service that I was getting and no longer needed the foot surgeon, I began going to a podiatrist closer to where I lived.

Well, I did the wrong thing. Somehow, I got a cut or scratch or something on the top of my right foot that I really hadn't paid any attention to. When I noticed, it had turned into a small sore, and I mentioned it to the podiatrist. He looked at it and put Betadine on it and told me to keep it clean and dry. I did that for a week or so and noticed that the area was getting larger, so I decided that I better go back to my trusted foot surgeon. I called and got an emergency visit for the next day.

When he examined my foot, he told me that I had a deep infection and that I needed to go home and pack a bag and report to the emergency room at the hospital that he worked out of in Virginia Beach, Virginia, right away. As usual, my sisters were with me, and we went to my house, packed a bag, and checked into the emergency room of the hospital that he told us to go to.

They were expecting me at the hospital and had a room ready. He had put in orders to immediately start IV antibiotics as well as oral antibiotics and to have a bone specialist and an infectious disease doctor to check my foot. His fear was that the infection had gone into the bone of my foot. If that was the case, that would not be a good thing.

They began IV antibiotics immediately as well as oral antibiotics. I had several tests done the next day, one of them being a bone scan. The Infectious Disease doctor told me that if the bone scan showed that there was an infection in the bone, they might have to amputate my foot because I had very poor circulation in my foot. Blood flow is required for the antibiotics to be able to get in there and clear up the infection.

I began praying, "Oh Lord, please increase the blood flow in my foot so that the antibiotics can get in there and wipe out the infection that is deep in my foot. And Lord, please don't let it have reached the bone. Lord, I thank you in advance. " John 14:14 says:

"If ye shall ask any thing in my name, I will do it."

I was in the hospital for three weeks, aggressively receiving IV and oral antibiotics. Thank God the infection had not gotten into the bone. Lord, I thank you. Great is the faithfulness Lord unto me.

It was set up that upon my release, each time I went to my dialysis treatment for the next month, I would also receive IV antibiotics through my dialysis liquid that went into the machine as well as continue to take oral antibiotics. In addition, home health care nurses would come three times a week and dress the wound. I had a very serious infection going on.

It was an intense time and process, but thank you, Lord, for your healing. My foot completely healed, and there is only a small scarred area that indicated that there was ever a problem. To God be the glory!

My list of doctors was becoming rather lengthy. Let's review. First, I had a primary care physician. I now also had a podiatrist, a pulmonologist, a nephrologist, a retina specialist, a neurologist, a cardiologist, an infectious disease doctor, and a bone specialist. But, I thank you, God, you brought me through it all. Isaiah 53:5 says:

"But he was wounded for our transgressions, he was bruised for our iniquities: the chastisement of our peace was upon him; and with his stripes we are healed."

Thank you, Lord, for bringing me through all of this with a reasonable portion of health and strength remaining!

I am still on dialysis and entering my 16th year of treatment. I call it my part-time job, lol, because really it is! I also walk with a walker now because I have arthritis in my knees, and I'm very unsteady on my feet. I also just had my second surgery for carpal tunnel in my hands. I had the right one done about two years ago. The left one was done in November of 2020.

I had a cataract growing in my good eye for the past couple of years, but they did not want to bother it until absolutely necessary since that was my only good eye. They said that they would monitor its growth, and when it became too obstructive to my vision, they would remove it then. When I went for that examination, I also was told that I had a scarred cornea and surgery would be needed on my cornea before they could remove the cataract.

On June 19, 2020, I had surgery on my cornea to remove the scarring. I must add here that this procedure was done after testing negative for Covid-19. At that time, as now, we were in the midst of a coronavirus pandemic. It is a requirement to be tested for Covid before proceeding with any scheduled surgeries. Thank you, Lord, for the negative result. Psalm 91:10-11 says:

> "There shall no evil befall thee, neither shall any plague come nigh thy dwelling. For he shall give his angels charge over thee, to keep thee in all thy ways."

The cornea surgery was successful. In the meantime, the cataract had grown to the point of needing to be removed. It was really obstructing the vision that I did have. Because that was the same eye that was healing, the cataract could not be removed until proper healing of the cornea had occurred.

It is a slow process, but after a few months, the cornea had healed enough, and cataract surgery was performed on December 18, 2020. That in itself was a miracle because I had originally been told that the surgery would have to wait to at least May, which would have been another five months. The reason for that was because of the pandemic, operating rooms were booked to the fullest, and cataract surgery was not considered a priority. John 14:27 says:

> "Peace I leave with you, my peace I give unto you: not as the world giveth, give I unto you. Let not your heart be troubled, neither let it be afraid."

I cried right there at the appointment desk when the scheduler told me that. I told her, "Miss, please see if something can be done. I really cannot see well, only have one eye that I rely on, and I will be blind by May." She went to talk to her supervisor and came back and told me that she was told to put me on the waiting list for cancellations. If one occurred, then I could fill in that slot.

Well, you can't tell me that God is not a miracle worker because when I went home that day, I began calling my prayer warriors to pray with me and pray that my vision would be corrected very soon.

About a week later, I got a call with a date for the surgery and all of my pre-opt information. "Won't He do it?" After having my third Covid-19 test because I also had to have one before my surgery on my hand and one before my cataract surgery. I again tested negative and was able to have my cataract surgery. Mark 9:23 says:

> "Jesus said unto him, if thou canst believe, all things are possible to him that believeth."

To God be the glory! There are still some issues being addressed with my cornea, but I thank God that I have more clarity of vision than I have had in a long time. Thank you, Lord!

These last few years have been challenging physically, but God has kept me through it all! My faith has been consistent because I know that God's promises are true. He has proven it over and over again. Lord, I thank you!

Walking by faith through the fires

Fire number 1:

One Wednesday evening in 2003, I was in my bedroom lying on the bed watching TV. My son had come in there with me and had fallen asleep. All of a sudden, I smelled smoke. I began looking around to see if I could see anything burning because the scent was very strong. I saw sparks across the room where there was a recliner in the corner and a pole lamp. Shaking my son, I told him to wake up quickly because something was burning.

Suddenly, we saw flames start to ignite the window curtains on that side of the room. Shaking Tyler hard because he was a deep sleeper, I told him to "Get up! We've got to get out of here. The room is on fire!"

Grabbing him and my cell phone, we ran out of the bedroom, into the living room, and out of the front door. As we were making our way to the front door, I saw flames flare up behind us, coming from the bedroom. In my haste, I did not think about closing the bedroom door. I was only thinking about getting out of there.

It was pouring down raining outside, but we had no time to grab a coat or anything. Tyler had on pajamas and socks, and I had on a lounging robe and footies on my feet. Tyler was crying, and I was trying to calm him down and comfort him, even as I felt like my heart was beating out of my chest. We made it out of the house and to the sidewalk as I called 911.

I also called my sisters and my brother. My son and I were standing outside in the pouring rain, getting drenched and in a state of shock.

The fire engines came quickly. My next-door neighbors must have heard the ruckus because they came out and told us to come inside their house.

In the meantime, my sisters, brother, and brother-in-law were also pulling up. The neighbor invited them into the house also.

As the firemen were battling the blaze, my Pastor at the time drove up. He was at church at prayer service, and someone had passed the news on to him. He came by to make sure that we were okay and didn't need anything. He also offered to pray with us and provide moral support for us. I appreciated this more than he could imagine. Ephesians 4:11-12 says:

> "And he gave some apostles; and some prophets; and some evangelists; and some, pastors and teachers; for the perfecting of the saints, for the work of the ministry, for the edifying of the body of Christ."

This man really was an awesome pastor. He was always there for all of his members. No matter what they needed. I was later told he had left the prayer meeting early, leaving one of the Deacons in charge so that he could come and see about us.

We were looking out of the door of our neighbor's house, watching the firemen as they battled the blaze, so we saw the Pastor walking up to the fireman left at the truck, who pointed out where we were. So he came next door, and the neighbor invited him in also.

I am so thankful for having a good relationship with our neighbors. Some people don't even know their neighbors.

The fire was extinguished, and the fireman came next door to let us know what was going on. They didn't really know the source yet but said someone would be out the next day to see if the source could be determined.

Pastor prayed with all of us who were there in the house that night and said that he would be back in the morning to help us get anything out of the house that was salvageable.

In the meantime, my son and I went home with one of my sisters for the night. Psalms 121:7-8 says:

> "The LORD shall preserve thee from all evil: he shall preserve thy soul. The Lord shall preserve thy going out and thy coming in from this time forth, and even forevermore."

Thank you, Lord, for preserving us!

I called the insurance company and scheduled a time to meet the adjuster at the house the next day. The fire marshal came while we were there to try to locate the source.

My bedroom and the back of the house were pretty much demolished. We were able to salvage some of my son's clothes and a couple of pieces of furniture from his room. Most of my clothes were scorched or water damaged, and my bedroom furniture was not salvageable at all.

We would not be able to move back in for at least a month because of all the repairs that had to be done. The fire marshal concluded that the fire started from the recliner sitting on the cord to the pole lamp. Evidently, the cord had become frayed by the recliner moving back and forth on it when it was sat in. I was not aware that the chair was even on the cord, but that was a lesson learned.

My sister that was a year older than me, invited my son and me to stay with her, her husband, and her children until we could get back into our house. They had an extra room and said it would not be a problem. Lord, I thank you. You always make a way! Philippians 4:19 says:

> "But my God shall supply all your needs according to his riches in glory by Christ Jesus."

We stayed with my sister and her family and were able to move back into the house in about a month. We stopped by several times to see what was being done as far as repairs.

After moving back in, we had to replace some furniture and clothing, but we were thankful that we had escaped with our lives. In moments while reflecting over the whole incident, I stopped to offer another prayer of thanksgiving to God. I thanked him that Herbert was already home in Heaven with him during this time because, in all reality, I don't know if I would have been able to get all of us out of the house safely. I would have been trying to help Herbert, who moved extremely slow and trying to encourage Tyler to go on outside, which he would have been afraid to do.

He had already been crying and afraid as it was dark outside. I know he wouldn't have left. He would have been trying to help me with his Dad. That was always what he did when I was trying to help Herbert walk. He would see me holding one arm, trying to steady him, and he would always grab the other arm, saying, "I've got you, Dad." I thank the Lord that my husband was already safe in his arms.

Fire number 2:

I still remember the date; September 25, 2019, as if it were yesterday, as it was the day after my birthday. By then, I was living in a senior apartment community. Tyler was about to graduate from college and had his own apartment in Richmond, Virginia.

That evening, I had gone into the kitchen to prepare dinner. My friend was in the back watching television. As I went into the kitchen, I heard someone banging on my apartment door.

Opening the door, I saw a lady looking very upset, telling me that she lived downstairs directly under me, and saying that her balcony was on fire. And that the flames were traveling up to my balcony. I looked out of the living room window because you could see my balcony through the living room, from the kitchen. Seeing flames rising up, I dialed 911.

I yelled for my friend to come up front because the balcony was on fire, and we needed to get out of there. He ran into the living room and out through the balcony door in an attempt to extinguish the flames that had already ignited my balcony furniture.

I began yelling for him to come back inside as it was too dangerous out there! He either couldn't hear me or thought that he could handle the situation. Crying, I went to the door, hoping that he could hear me as I screamed, "We have got to get out of here! Come on NOW!"

He finally came in just as the living room window burst, and the sprinklers came on, spraying water everywhere.

All this was happening on the day after my 62nd birthday. Remember, I was living in a senior community. I'd had to move out of my home three years prior to that because I had developed arthritis in my knees really bad and could no longer safely manage going up and down the steps required to enter and exit my house. I was also now walking with a walker and could not move quickly.

My friend also could not move that fast either. He had been a dialysis patient for 36 years and wasn't that steady on his feet either. As we left the apartment and closed the door, we started banging on our neighbors' doors, alerting them that there was a fire in the building.

Our next-door neighbor, in the meantime, had seen the flames on her balcony also, and she was in the hallway. She had forgotten to grab her walker or her cane. I grabbed her and told her to hold onto one side of my walker. I already had my friend holding onto the other side of my walker. So I was in the middle, and we were all moving down the hall just as quickly as we could, still banging on doors alerting people as we went.

I lived on the third floor, and the elevators were inoperable on my end of the building. My prayer was, "Lord, please help us to get out of here safely. If we have to manipulate the stairs, please keep each of us safe and not let us fall."

My neighbor was older than I, and she was really panicked, which was understandable. I could also see my friend was getting tired, and so was I. However, I was trying to the best of my ability to encourage the three of us. Psalms 91:4 says:

"He shall cover thee with his feathers, and under his wings shalt thou trust: his truth shall be thy shield and buckler."

There was a staircase right by my apartment because I lived at the end of the hallway. However, I told my friend and my neighbor that we needed to go towards the opposite end of the building from where the fire was because it was going to take us a while to get down the stairs. And, if we were at the opposite end of the building, it would take the fire longer to get down there. By then, hopefully, the fireman would have it contained before it got that far. I could feel my heart pounding in my chest as I was trying my best to be strong for the three of us.

It was a very large apartment complex. It had a north side, a central area, and a south side. I lived on the north side. We continued walking as fast as we could, still on the third-floor level. Soon, we saw a fireman up on that level knocking on doors and making sure that everyone was getting out of the building.

They told us if we continued walking that the elevator on the south side of the building could be used. Glory to God! We were almost there! We would not have to try to manage the stairs. God is so good! We made it to the south side of the building and were able to catch the elevator down to the ground floor. Look at God! Won't HE do it? Yes, He will!

Outside, several people had gathered. My neighbor and I found a bench to sit on, and my friend sat on my walker seat. As firemen were going in and out of the building, one of them noticed my friend's knee on his left leg. He had on shorts and evidently had gotten a burn on his leg when he was trying to extinguish the fire on the balcony. He did not even realize that he was burned. He said he did not feel anything, and I had not noticed because I was so busy trying to get us out of there.

They had a paramedic come and look at his leg and put a temporary dressing on it. They then took him to an ambulance to be transported to the hospital. In the midst of this, I had called my sisters as well as my friend's daughter and sisters to let them know what was going on. As usual, my sisters came to my aid, as well as my pastor and his wife.

This was a different pastor from the one during the first fire. God has truly blessed our church with faithful pastors who have a love and heart for their membership. For that, I am thankful.

All these people were trying to get to me but were unable to because the streets and the surrounding area had been blocked off. The apartment complex was very large, and they were evacuating everyone for safety reasons.

It ended up being a multiple-fire engine situation. So there were several engines out there from several firehouses. I had never seen that many fire engines in one place before. I began praying, "Lord, please take care of everyone and don't let anyone be seriously injured. And please let my friend's injury be minor."

They also had buses out there for residents who could not stand long and needed to sit down until the word was given that it was safe to go back inside. I was pushed on my walker by a paramedic down the block to where my sister had been instructed to drive her vehicle and wait for me. Before I left, my neighbor's daughter and grandson had come to get her, so

I was glad of that because I did not want to leave her without knowing that she was okay.

My sister took me to the hospital to check on my friend. When I arrived, some of his family members were already there. I went into the treatment area to see about him and was told that they were going to keep him at least overnight, or maybe for a day or two because he had a pretty bad burn on his left knee and thigh area. They wanted to make sure that proper wound care was started and that no infection set in.

I left the hospital with my sisters and spent the night with my oldest sister. I was in disbelief. My thoughts were here I am again, Lord, involved in another fire. Finding myself in need of a place to stay once again. Philippians 4:6 says:

> "Be careful for nothing; but in everything by prayer and supplication with thanksgiving, let your requests be made known unto God."

The next morning, once again, I called my insurance adjuster. Then I called my sisters, who went with me to the apartment complex, to see if there were any clothes that were salvageable because I only had on what I had left in that night. I was able to get a few items of clothing that had not been smoked up or water damaged too badly.

I also went to the apartment complex office and spoke to the property manager. I was told that all of the apartments on my end of the building from my floor all the way down to the first floor, and about three apartments over, would have to be totally gutted, so it would be about three months before I could get back in.

I called the insurance company to let them know my situation so that they could put me up in a hotel. I wasn't able to stay with either of my sisters as they both had steps, and I could not manipulate steps anymore.

It was no problem as the insurance company was very accommodating and put me up in a very nice hotel suite for the length of time that I needed.

Thank God I did not have to worry about my son during this time because he was away at college. Of course, I had to call him with the news, and he was very concerned. He came home that weekend to check on me and felt better after he saw that I was okay.

My friend was released from the hospital after a couple of days, and he was okay. He had to have home health care to dress his wounds three times a week. The area healed well, and he was doing okay after that.

There were some things that were salvageable, not a lot, but some. None of the furniture was much good because of either fire, smoke, or water damage. Clothes that were in my walk-in closet, and some of the items that were in the closet in my bathroom, and my linen closet, were salvageable.

Periodically, I checked back with the complex's office. I was told that the move back-in-time had been extended due to the extent of the work that had to be done.

My conversations with God became, "Lord, first, I thank you for sparing my life. Now, Lord, I need you to show me what to do. I cannot live in this hotel long-term. Lord, please put me where you will have me to be."

My friend's daughter researched some senior living communities for me. We called and got information on a few of them and if they had any openings. She was kind enough to take me to visit some of those places and get applications.

After visiting some of the apartments and getting brochures and information on others, I settled on one that I really, really liked.

The one that I truly wanted was an exercise in faith for me for a couple of reasons. First of all, they had no vacancies right then and would not have any until December. This was the first of October. Secondly, it was a little more expensive than I was used to paying.

My prayer was, "Dear Lord, I am putting this in your hands. You place me where you would have me to be. You are Jehovah Jireh, my provider. I trust You, Lord."

Of all the places that I had seen or looked at in the brochures, I knew the one that I desired, but I had to see if it was what God desired for me. This place that I desired was a beautiful place. It was a senior luxury apartment with two bedrooms, two full bathrooms, one of which had a walk-in shower which is what I truly needed, a gym, a swimming pool, a library, a computer room, a billiards room, and a clubhouse. So, I put in my application and left it in God's hands. Proverbs 3:5-6 says:

> "Trust in the LORD with all thine heart; and lean not unto thine own understanding. In all thy ways acknowledge him, and he shall direct thy paths."

Guess what? I got approved for the place. I moved in the Saturday before Christmas in 2019. God is so good! He is so faithful! And once again, Jehovah-Jireh, my provider, all of the material things that I lost were replaced by insurance. However, some of the more sentimental things, such as pictures, items, and mementos, could not be replaced. Still, the memories associated with those things were forever etched in my heart. God, I thank you!

1 Peter 5:6-7 says:

> "Humble yourselves therefore under the mighty hand of God, that he may exalt you in due time: Casting all your care upon him; for He careth for you."

Lord, thank you for your exultation and your due time! Your timing is perfect. You may not come when we always want you to, but you are always right on time.

Walking by faith through a second chance at love

Eddie

God has everything in our lives already planned out for us, and often we don't even realize it. This became quite obvious to me in January of 2012.

By this time, I had been a widow for ten years. I had not had a date or been in any kind of relationship since my husband's death. Not because I had not had offers, but because I was solely concentrating on raising my son and getting him prepared to go to college.

I was also determined that my son would not see me dating different men and going out and things like that during this time of my life. My focus was solely on him.

I had always said that I could not see myself falling in love again because my husband and I had such a beautiful relationship. I could not imagine anything that could match up to that. I certainly was not looking for a man; that's not something that I'd ever done. God always sent the man to me! Well, it seemed His plan was coming to fruition, and I had no idea.

I had been going to the same dialysis center since September of 2005. However, I had been on the second shift. I would go in at 9 a.m. and get out of my treatment at about 1:15 pm. I would sometimes see people from the first shift leaving as I was coming in.

Well, it turned out there was someone that God wanted me to get to know. I had put my name on the waiting list to move to the early morning shift because I am a morning person. I like to get up and get things done and get them out of the way. My son was about to go off to college, so there was no need for me to be home in the morning anymore like I was when I was seeing him off to school.

Around the month of November 2011, I got the opportunity to start on the early morning shift. My new time was 5:15 am. My treatment lasted four hours and fifteen minutes. That's a long time to sit in a chair in one position and just watch TV, and there was no guarantee that I was going to fall asleep each time.

To keep myself entertained, I took word search puzzle books and worked on puzzles during my treatment. I didn't really know anyone on the early morning shift, but being the friendly person that I am, I would speak to whomever I saw and sometimes just have a polite conversation or small talk.

Periodically, they would change our seating arrangement at dialysis for one reason or another.

After being on the early shift for about a month, my seat was changed. I went to my chair as usual and got situated. Once I was put on the machine, I opened up my puzzle book and began working on my puzzles. I heard the person next to me say, "Good morning." I looked up and over, and I said, "Oh, good morning. How are you?"

He said, "I'm fine. Are you on this shift now?"

"Yes, I am," I replied. "What time do you come in?"

"My chair time is 5 a.m.," was his response.

"Oh, so you are one of the first ones that they put on here?" I asked.

"Yes, I've been here long enough to earn that privilege," he replied.

"Oh, okay," I responded as I went back to working on my puzzles. He finished his treatment before I did, and when he got up to leave, he said, "Well, you have a good day now."

I said, "Okay, you do the same."

Each treatment after that, I noticed that I was sitting in the same chair which was next to this man. One day he asked me, "How long does it take you to do one of those puzzles?" I told him it depended on how difficult the puzzle was, so the amount of time varied. We just continued to chit-chat periodically for several weeks.

I noticed that this man was very friendly to a lot of the people there. Everyone seemed to know him. He would go by different people's chairs, speak to them, and ask how they were doing on his way out from time to time.

One Friday, he came up to my chair directly and told me to have a good weekend. He also asked me did I have any plans for the weekend. I told him nothing that I could think of, only going to church because I go to Sunday school and church every Sunday. At that time, I was one of the teachers of the women's Sunday school class. I thoroughly enjoyed it, so that was something that I looked forward to. Hebrews 10: 25 says:

> "Not forsaking the assembling of ourselves together, as the manner of some is; but exhorting one another: and so much the more, as ye see the day approaching."

I always looked forward to weekly fellowshipping with my church family.

Several weeks passed with the same scenario. Just small talk and chit-chat, and on Friday, stopping by the chair with the same question. "What are your plans for the weekend?" He would ask. And I had the same response, "Just Sunday school and church."

I was a person who prided myself on inviting people to my church. So, one day as we were chit-chatting, he said, "You go to church every Sunday? What church do you go to?" I told him the name of my church was First Baptist Church of Logan Park. I also told him if he wasn't doing anything some Sundays, to feel free to come and join us. I told him we had a welcoming and loving congregation, and we would love to have him and his family visit with us.

I told him if he didn't know where it was, I would be glad to give him the address. And if he needed transportation, we had a church bus, or I could pick him and his family up since it would be their first time coming.

I asked, "How many of you all would it be? And do you have a wife and children?" He told me that he didn't have a wife, but he had a daughter, but she was grown and living on her own. He added that she was active in her own church, so it was just him.

I said, "Okay, just let me know. I also pick up my sister for church. She lives five minutes from me, and I wanted to make sure that there is enough room if you and your family want to go." He replied, thank you, and that he might just take me up on that, and then he left.

The next week, things changed a bit. It seemed that we were talking a little bit more. One day, during the week, he came over to my chair and asked would I like to go to lunch one day the next week. I was kind of surprised. He seemed to be a nice enough man, so I said yes. He asked if I wanted to go next Thursday, and I agreed because I didn't have anything planned. He said he would be looking forward to it and left.

Suddenly, tears began rolling down my cheeks. I didn't know how I felt. I texted my sisters and told them that I was crying, and they wanted to know why? I told them because I was just asked out on a date. They thought that crying because of that was funny.

I explained that I hadn't been out with any man other than my husband in over 30 years. I had been married to Herbert for 20 years, and I had been a widow for ten years. I know that we were just going out as friends, but it would be kind of awkward because this was not a man that I knew, and I had not dated in so long that it felt kind of weird. I told them that I would call them later when I got home.

This was not like when I had been approached before, and my response was always a polite "no thank you." I took the time right in my dialysis chair to talk to God. I said something to the effect of "God, what's going on? I invited this man to church, and now he invites me to lunch? Are you trying to tell me something, Lord? You did not allow me to hesitate or turn this man down when he asked me out. What is happening here?"

Tyler did not have much longer left in high school then. He would be going off to college soon, and maybe God did not want me to be lonely.

I told God, as usual, that I was putting it in his hands and to please order my steps. Jeremiah 29:11 says:

"For I know the thoughts that I think toward you, saith the LORD, thoughts of peace, and not of evil, to give you an expected end."

Well, Thursday, January 5, 2012, came. I will never forget the date because that was the date that we both realized that we wanted to be very good friends, and could possibly be good company for each other. Now God had to be in that, because how many first dates can you go on and feel so comfortable and at ease as if you have known this person for a long time?

We discovered that we had a lot in common. I knew his name was Eddie from hearing people talk to him and refer to him at dialysis. I didn't know him like that, so I used to call him Mr. Eddie.

I found out that day that he did not like that. I told him I was only trying to be respectful. He made me laugh because he frowned his face up and said, "I'm not that much older than you!" That became a joke between us because every now and then, I would throw in Mr. in front of Eddie, and we would just laugh.

At lunch, we sat and talked for a couple of hours, then sat and talked some more once in the car. Before we parted, he told me that he would love to go to church with me. I told him that was great and we would plan for that. Later that evening, he called me, and we talked some more.

After that initial date, we talked every day at least two or three times a day. He called me every morning when he first got up to say good morning, even though he was going to see me on dialysis days. And he called every night before he went to bed to say good night. We also talked on the phone several times between the "good mornings" and the "good nights."

That became our daily routine. Something else that became routine for us was prayer. We prayed with each other every morning before leaving our homes to go to dialysis. The good-morning calls became good morning prayer calls. We thanked God for allowing us to see another day and for a reasonable portion of health and strength.

We prayed for our fellow dialysis patients as well as the staff, and we prayed for one another. We also prayed that God would be in the midst of our relationship. Our prayer life with each other grew stronger and stronger, and we got along really well.

We eventually met each other's families, and the families got along very well. "Lord, I thank you. Everything is falling into place. It is nobody, but you Lord! "Ecclesiastes 4: 9-10 says:

> "Two are better than one; because they have a good reward for their labour. For if they fall, the one will lift up his fellow: but woe to him that is alone when he falleth; for he hath not another to help him up."

We were both so thankful to God for bringing us together.

Eddie and I also liked some of the same TV shows, so we would watch them together. Sometimes he'd watch them at his place, and I would watch at mine. When we weren't together in the same house on commercial breaks, we would call each other and talk about what was happening on the show.

We would also do little fun things like call each other in the morning and tell each other to get our coffee ready, so we could have coffee together. He would sip coffee at his place, and I would sip coffee at mine while we talked.

We decided that the fifth of every month would be our anniversary. None of us knows how long we have left to live, but we both knew being on dialysis that life wasn't guaranteed. We were going to live each day that we could, to the fullest.

So, the fifth of every month, or the day before, or the day after the fifth, if it fell on a dialysis day, we would go somewhere to eat and go to a movie. We always gave each other an anniversary card.

It was funny because, after a while, we ran out of a selection of anniversary cards by giving one every month and realized that we were repeating some of the cards that we had already bought for each other.

Eddie was kind, quiet, and a gentleman. He was also a simple man. He didn't require much. Material things for himself seemed to be unimportant to him, but he wanted me to have the world. He never went into a store and came out without something for me.

He knew that I was not a person that valued big expensive things. I like nice things, but it was the simple things in life that impressed me and made me happy. Just someone showing me that they were thinking of me was important to me.

And that's what he did. If he went into a store and saw a wind chime, he would buy it for me. He knew that I loved to hear the sound of the wind chimes when the wind blew. He purchased several and put them out on my back porch when I was living in the house. He also bought them for my balcony when I moved to my senior apartment. He loved to buy me little plaques and whatnots, picture frames, etc. And he loved to surprise me with flowers.

Our relationship quickly grew to one of mutual respect, caring, as well as love, and understanding. When I first met Eddie in 2012, he had already been on dialysis for 29 years! He told me how good God had been to him. I told him that he was a walking talking miracle that was favored by God! Psalms 5:12 says:

> "For thou, Lord, wilt bless the righteous; with favour, wilt thou compass him as with a shield."

Many doctors have also called him a miracle. You do not see too many people that have lived on dialysis that long. And once I started going to doctors' appointments with him, the doctors said that on a regular basis.

Eddie was my hero. He was my hero because I watched how he encouraged people at dialysis who sometimes wanted to give up. He used himself as an example of how you can have a long, productive life even being on dialysis. He was an encouragement to many patients, including me, because some days, I just did not want to go. He would tell me, "Baby, you've got to go. You don't want to make yourself sick."

I used to tell him all the time that I felt like God's purpose for his life was to be an encouragement to others. Even the nurses and doctors at the dialysis center said the same thing about Eddie. Philippians 2: 4 says:

> "Look not every man on his own things, but every man also on the things of others."

And Eddie was very compassionate about others.

Another thing I admired about this man was in all the years that I knew him, I never heard him complain about anything. I knew for a fact that he had many days of discomfort and not feeling well, yet he never complained. I can truly say that he lived by Philippians 4:11, which says:

> "Not that I speak in respect of want: for I have learned, in whatsoever state I am, therewith to be content."

And content and thankful was how he lived!

I knew this for it is what I had seen with my own eyes. Several people come to mind when I think of how he has helped them. There was one man, in particular, that was 88 years old. I knew it was hard for him being on dialysis and coming to his treatments. Every day, when he walked through the door, he would always say, "I hate this place."

He seemed very unhappy. He never smiled, never had a pleasant word, and just seemed so miserable. Everyone knew it and talked about it. But not my Eddie. Eddie picked up on that, and he began joking with the man. At first, he was very resistant, but Eddie was persistent, and they soon discovered a common ground.

Eddie had a joke about beans that he would always tell him, and he would just laugh! That did my heart good. I told Eddie whether he knew it or not, he was a blessing to that man because he brought some joy into his life. That man has since passed, but at least I know that he'd had some laughter before he left this world, and Eddie had been a big part of it.

There was another patient there who was also in his 80s. He happened to be one of my downstairs neighbors in my senior apartment building. One day, after his treatment, he was sitting in the lobby, and Eddie and I were talking to him. He asked me did I have any candy because his mouth was very dry. I searched through my purse, and I found a few pieces of hard candy. I gave them to him, and he was so thankful. He immediately opened the wrapper and put a piece in his mouth. Dry mouth is something that a lot of patients experience following their dialysis treatment because one of the things that the treatment does is remove excess fluid from the body.

To tell you the kind of person that Eddie was, the next time we went to the grocery store, he went to the candy aisle and bought a bag of hard candies for that patient. It became routine for him when he went to the grocery store to always purchase a bag of candy for this man. That is the kind of heart that he had. That man has also passed, but he was able to leave this world knowing that someone had cared enough about him to try to ease his discomfort. The Bible says in Matthew 5: 8:

"Blessed are the pure in heart: for they shall see God."

Eddie and I used to love going to the boardwalk at Ocean View Beach, watching the waves, enjoying the weather, and God's beautiful creation. Sometimes we would go out to the boat ramp and watch the men put their boats into water or their jet skis, kayaks and canoes.

Sometimes we would just go and sit in the park. He taught me how to appreciate the simple things in life.

Being around him always gave me a feeling of peace and contentment. I have never heard Eddie raise his voice or ever seen him angry. A very soft-spoken man, he did not like confrontation. His siblings would often tell me that when they were growing up, Eddie would disappear when the arguing and fussing started. He did not like being around strife and confusion. Matthew 5:9 says:

"Blessed are the peacemakers: for they shall be called the children of God."

Another thing Eddie taught me was that it does no good to get upset over things that you have no control over. He viewed this as a waste of time and energy.

Eddie and I had been a couple for about five years before some additional things started going wrong with his health. 2018 was a rather difficult year for him, and he had several health challenges and hospitalizations.

December of that year, I decided that I wanted to give Eddie a birthday party for his 70th birthday, which would be coming up in May of 2019. I wanted it to be a birthday celebration, but I also wanted it to be a celebration and a testament to the favor that God had placed on his life by allowing him to live so long on dialysis. I felt that this was a memorable event. Psalms 90:10 says:

> "The days of our years are threescore years and ten; and if by reason of strength they be fourscore years, yet is their strength labour and sorrow; for it is soon cut off, and we fly away."

One of the things that Eddie's daughter does is event planning, so I knew who to go to with my ideas of what I wanted. I told her my ideas and got her input as well. She knew whom to network with and what to do to plan the celebration. And plan we did.

The difficult part would be keeping it under wraps so that Eddie would not find out about it. I had to talk in code when I was on the telephone. Or text people or talk to them when I was away from him because Mr. Man didn't miss out on too much. Lol!

Fast forward to May 2019. One Saturday evening, at the Residence Inn by Marriott in Norfolk, Virginia, the 70th birthday celebration/36th year of life celebration on dialysis of

Eddie Taylor transpired. What a joyful time was had by all. And he was totally surprised. All of his family was there, as well as friends and some church members.

We were also honored by the presence of the director of his dialysis center for all of those years that he'd been a patient, even though she was retired at the time of the party. She cared that much about Eddie to take her time and attend.

Two of the registered nurses and the dietitian who had worked with him for so many years also attended. They all gave heartfelt comments about the years that they had worked with Eddie. It was a beautiful occasion. I thank God that he had the opportunity to experience that, and I thank God for placing the idea to do that for him on my heart.

Many people don't realize what a toll being on dialysis can take on your body. Later that year, Eddie began having health issues related to dialysis. He began falling periodically, at first. Then the falls became more frequent. This was due to his blood pressure dropping too low. With several of the falls, he'd obtained head injuries, some requiring stitches.

Eventually, it became safer for him to use a cane to help with his balance. A few months after that, he began using a wheelchair. He also began having issues with the arm and hand that they had been using for his dialysis treatments for all those years. After a period of time, his appetite was not good, and he began losing a lot of weight. One thing after another occurred. Eventually, he became very weak and lost the ability to ambulate at all. He was also hospitalized several times during his last two years of life.

He was in the hospital on Thanksgiving of 2019. At that time, we had been together every holiday since January of 2012, no exceptions. So, I was not about to let this holiday be any different just because he was in the hospital. I ordered a full Thanksgiving dinner from Cracker Barrel, and I fixed a plate for him, and my best friend was kind enough to take the time out of her holiday to take me to the hospital to share Thanksgiving dinner with him there. She also went up to speak to him to see how he was feeling and then left us alone to celebrate. She told me to give her a call when I was ready to leave. Matthew 22:39 says:

> "And the second (commandment) is like unto it, Thou shalt love thy neighbour as thyself."

This was the same best friend that you read about in one of my previous chapters. She has always been there for me, and I for her. Thank God for true friends!

Eddie's condition improved enough for him to be discharged. As time passed, he began to get weaker and weaker, but he was able to sit up in his wheelchair and have Christmas dinner. He had requested Cornish hens, so that is what I prepared as well as a multitude of other things. He was able to eat reasonably well and seemed to enjoy it.

He also set up for almost two hours, which was exceptional for him at that point in time. He seemed to enjoy Christmas, for which I was grateful.

January 5th, 2020, was our eight-year anniversary. Unable to go out and celebrate, we simply enjoyed being in each other's company and reminiscing about all of the fun times and previous years that we'd had together. We definitely took time on that day to hold hands and thank God for giving us the eight wonderful years that he had given us.

As the month progressed, Eddie began to get weaker and had no appetite at all. Attempts at dialysis were hard to manage because his blood pressure was consistently low, and they had problems bringing it back up. He ended up back in the hospital on Monday, January 27th. He was transported by ambulance to the Emergency Room from dialysis because his blood pressure was so low that they could not perform his dialysis. The doctors told his daughter, who was always by his bedside day and night whenever he was hospitalized, that it was time to notify the family to come and say their final goodbyes.

That Eddie was well-loved was quite obvious by the parade of people that came to the hospital to show their love. He had five surviving sisters, who all had children and grandchildren. They were all there. It was a bitter, sweet time. That Tuesday, January 28th, they all came to see him, and he was able to respond to most of them in his own way. When they left, his daughter stepped out, and I had my time with him.

I told him how much I loved him and how he had enriched my life over the past eight years. And that I hope the past eight years of his life had been just as enriching and happy and full of love for him as he had made them for me.

I told him that I did not want him to suffer and that I would be fine. That his daughter would be fine, and all his family would be fine. I told him that when God called him, to go and claim his well-deserved reward. To go and be with his Mom and Dad, to go and be with his four brothers. He was the fifth and final brother to leave this earth. My heart was breaking, but I could not let him see that, so God gave me the strength to endure.

About 6:30 a.m. on Thursday, January 30, 2020, his daughter called me and told me that he had taken his last breath and gone on peacefully. John 14:18 says:

"I will not leave you comfortless: I will come to you."

And he did. God came to me during that time, and even though I was quite sad, he gave me peace and comfort.

God, I thank you for answering Eddie's prayers. He had faith and believed that you would not allow him to suffer. He had always told me that he did not want to suffer and that he wanted to pass peacefully in his sleep, which he had. Lord, thank you for your grace and mercy in granting Eddie's request. Lord, thank you for your faithfulness.

Lord, thank you for allowing me to experience the love, kindness, gentleness, and genuine caring from this sweet man who had occupied my life for the past eight years. It was only you that made this relationship possible and brought it to fruition. He will always occupy a special place in my heart. I love and miss you, "my Eddie."

EPILOGUE

Writing this book has not been an easy task. With my visual impairment, it was sometimes quite difficult. I have also had hospitalization and surgeries since its inception.

I sometimes became frustrated and wondered would I ever be able to complete this project. However, God placed a wonderful young lady in my life (my Eddie's daughter). I call her my "daughter in love." She has been instrumental in setting up my computer and finding the equipment that I needed to make the computer more user-friendly for me with my visual issues.

In actuality, I initially wrote the whole book on my Android phone. It was easier because I could put the phone right up to my face and do what I needed to do. When it came time to review it and make revisions, I used the adaptations that had been made to the computer.

With her help and my belief in Philippians 4:13, God made it possible! Philippians 4:13 says:

"I can do all things through Christ which strengtheneth me."

This is something that I have wanted to do for years, but God showed me that this was the right time. Events have constantly unfolded in my life at such a time as this, which enabled me to put together a "testimonial journey of my life." In the midst of its trials and hardships, I made it by my faith and God's grace. I am hoping that my story will be a vessel of *Hope*, *Encouragement*, and *Inspiration* to someone who may be facing difficult times. Always remember, God is able, and His word is true. Nothing is impossible with God. I am a living, breathing, walking, and talking witness!

Whatever situations we encounter in our lives, there is an answer on how to get through them throughout the Bible. Just keep the faith, and God will see you through!

Just trust Him. And hold onto your faith1 Wishing you much love and blessings to all!! God, I thank you!

About the Author

Trudy Eileen Nelson Stiff was born in Norfolk, Virginia. An alumnus of Virginia State University in Petersburg, Virginia, she majored in Special Education with a concentration of working with the Emotionally Disturbed (ED).

Employed for 36 years by the Commonwealth of Virginia at Southeastern Virginia Training Center, she began her career as a Developmental Aide. After a short period of time, she was promoted to supervisor of her shift. Later, she applied and was chosen for a supervisory position, where she was promoted to supervisor of a residential building. She retired in 2016 as a Human Services Care Supervisor. Mrs. Stiff is a widow and the mother of two children, one of whom is deceased.

Mrs. Stiff is a long-time member of the First Baptist Church of Logan Park, also located in Norfolk, Virginia. Raised in this church, it is dear to her heart. As such, she has dedicated her time and services in many capacities to this church.

She speaks highly of the religious background and training that she received from her parents as well as other members of the church as she grew in her faith. She often says, "There is nothing like the wisdom derived from the Elders of the church. Thank you, Lord, for their wisdom, and thank you, Lord, for bringing me this far by faith!"

www.ingramcontent.com/pod-product-compliance
Lightning Source LLC
Chambersburg PA
CBHW072039080526
44578CB00007B/326